Draw, DOODLE, Design

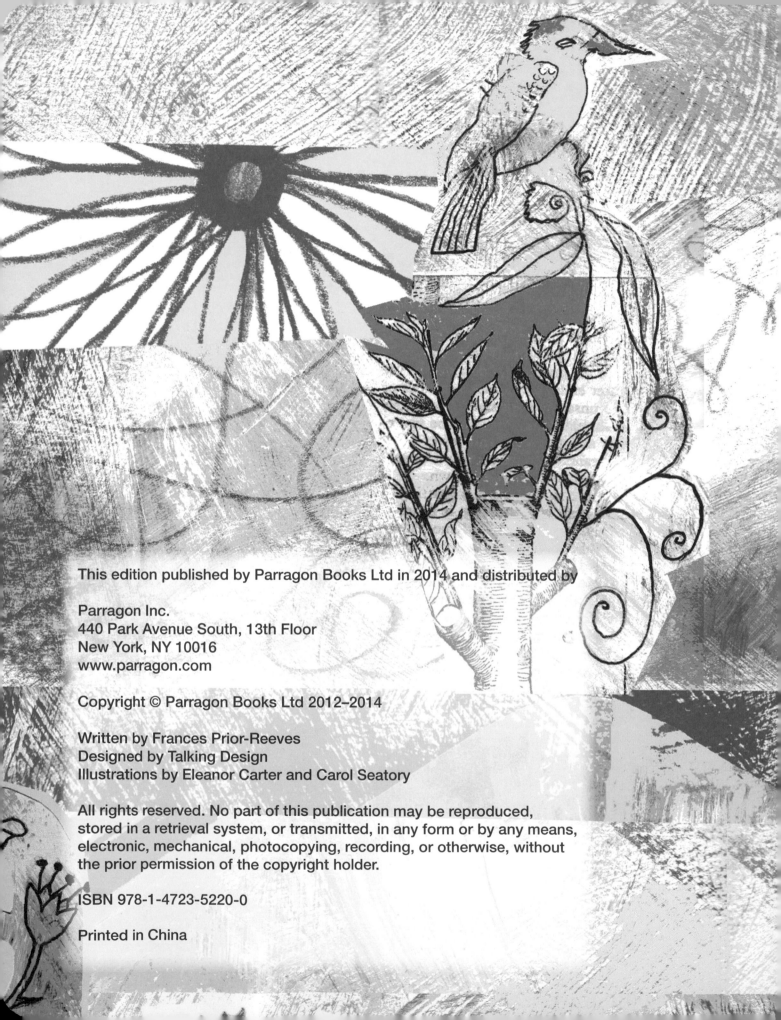

This edition published by Parragon Books Ltd in 2014 and distributed by

Parragon Inc.
440 Park Avenue South, 13th Floor
New York, NY 10016
www.parragon.com

Written by Frances Prior-Reeves
Designed by Talking Design
Illustrations by Eleanor Carter and Carol Seatory

ISBN 978-1-4723-5220-0

Printed in China

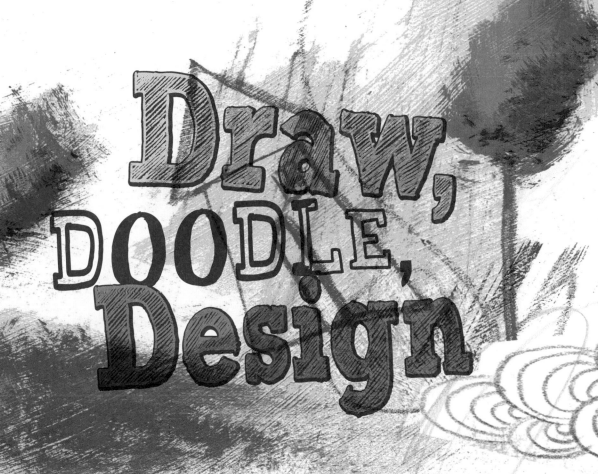

Draw, DOODLE, Design

PaRragon

Bath • New York • Cologne • Melbourne • Delhi
Hong Kong • Shenzhen • Singapore • Amsterdam

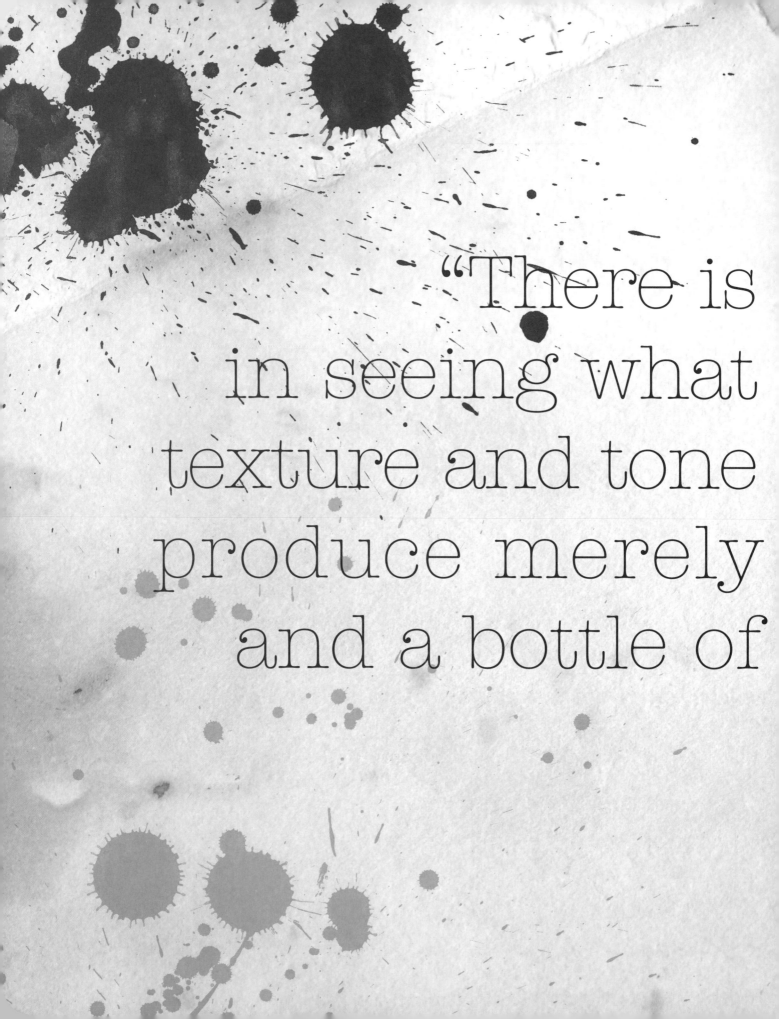

"There is in seeing what texture and tone produce merely and a bottle of

something magical
you can do; what
and color you can
with a pen point
ink." **Ida Rentoul Outhwaite.**

Fill this page with circles.
Can you see a pattern within your image?

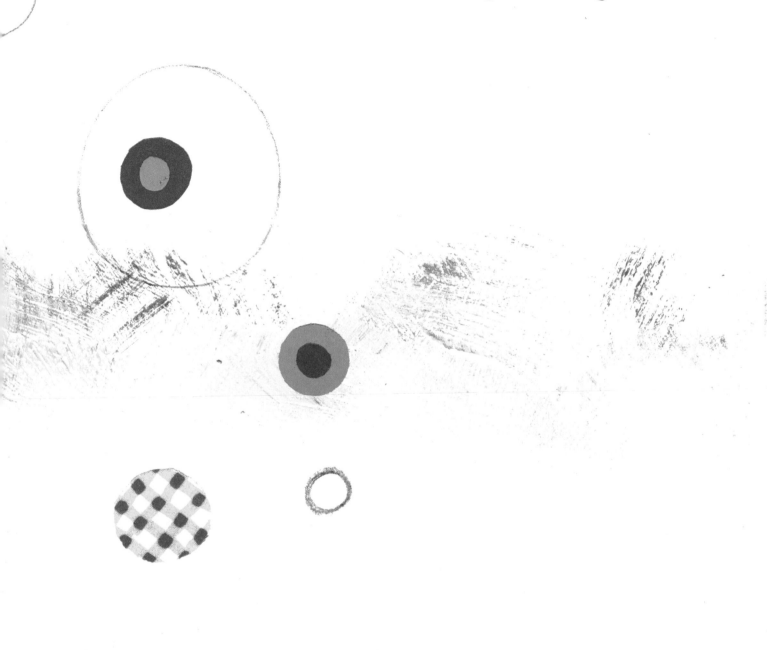

Fill this page with **SQUARES.**
How is your pattern different?

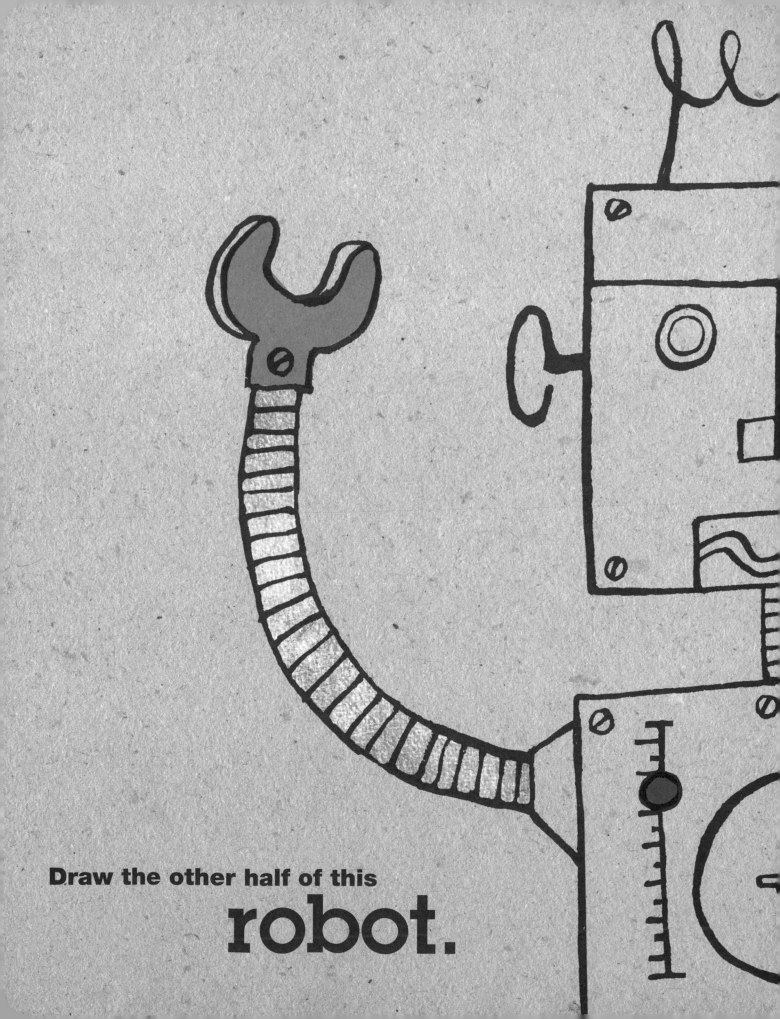

Draw the other half of this
robot.

Fill these pages with your

doodles.

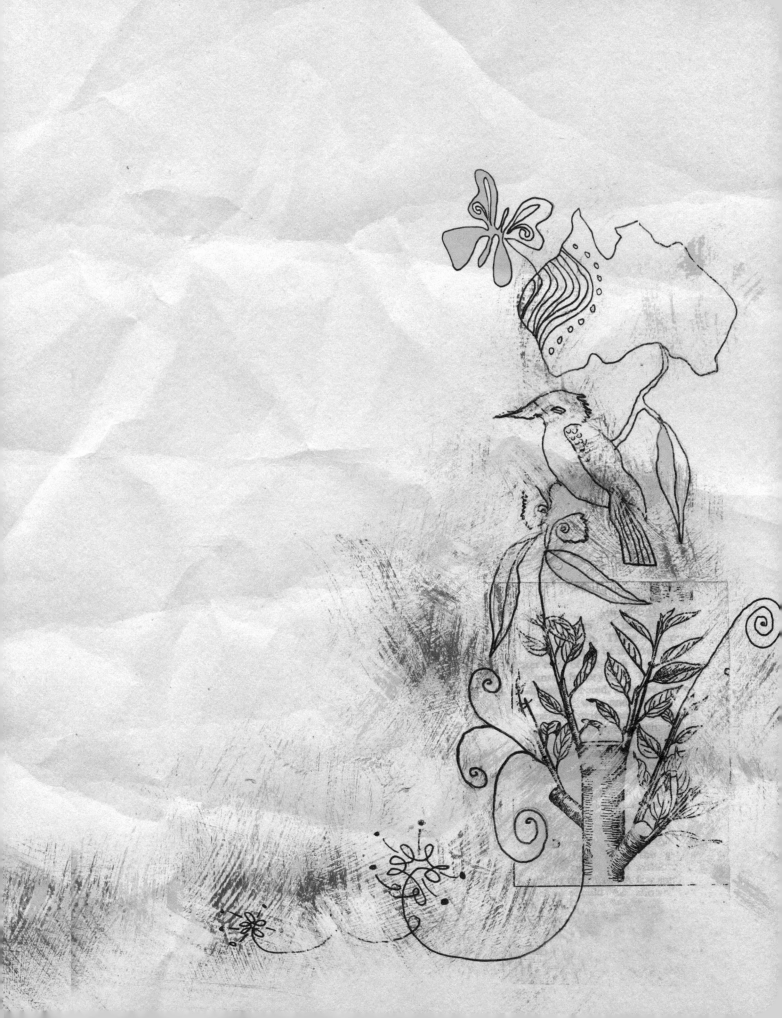

Draw your favorite
mythical creature.

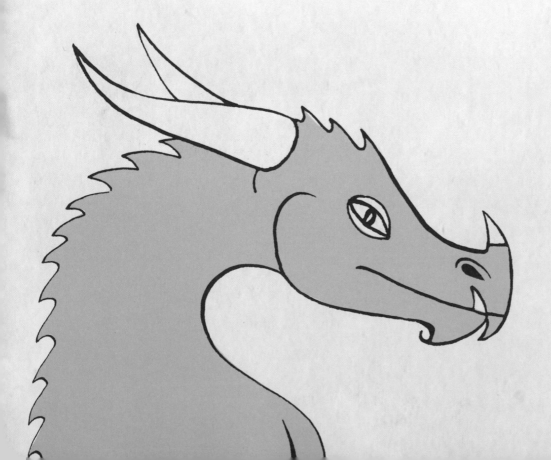

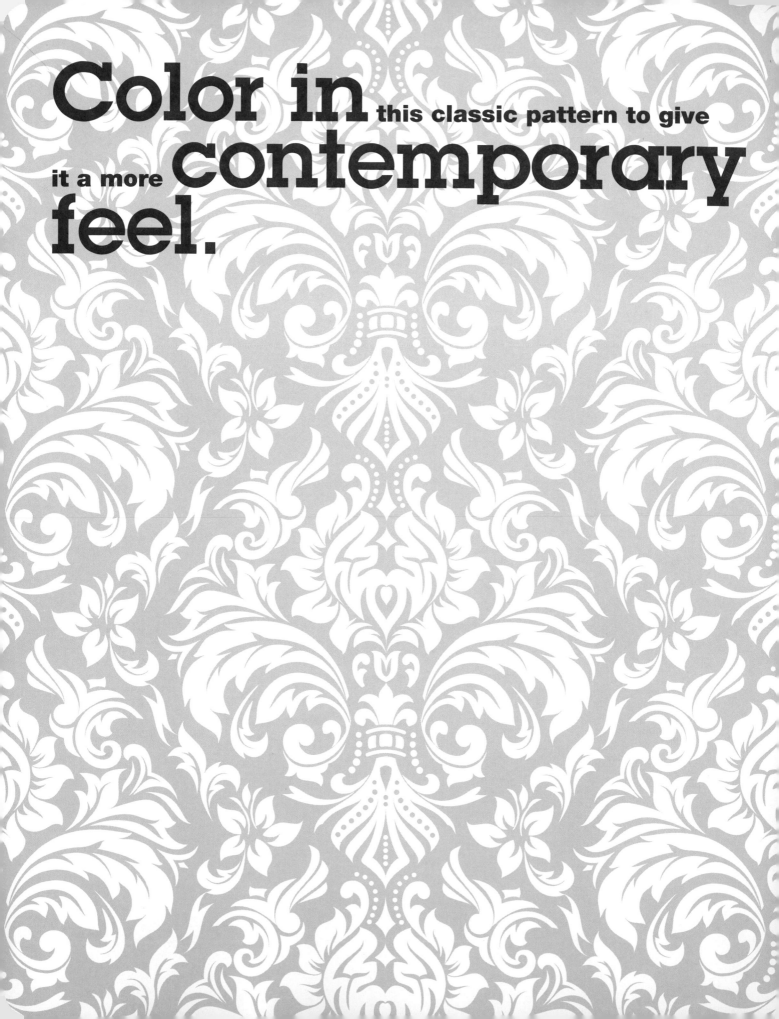

Color in this classic pattern to give it a more contemporary feel.

List the **SEVEN COLORS** of the rainbow from your favorite to your least favorite. What does your personal rainbow look like? Draw it.

B

G

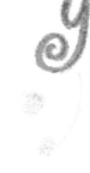
O

Y

R

Red,
Orange,
Yellow,
Green,
Blue,
Indigo,
Violet.

Add your own design to this
vase.

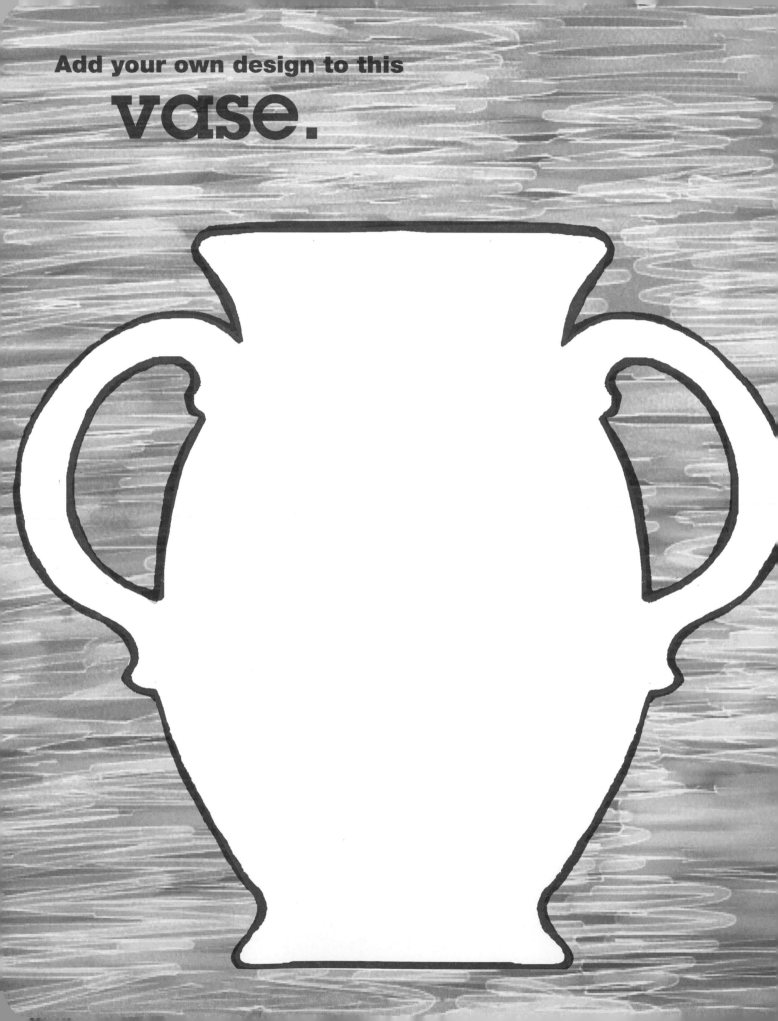

Fill these shelves.

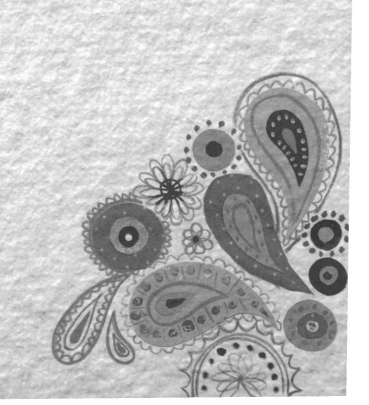

"Color is my obsession, joy,

day-long
and torment."

Claude Monet.

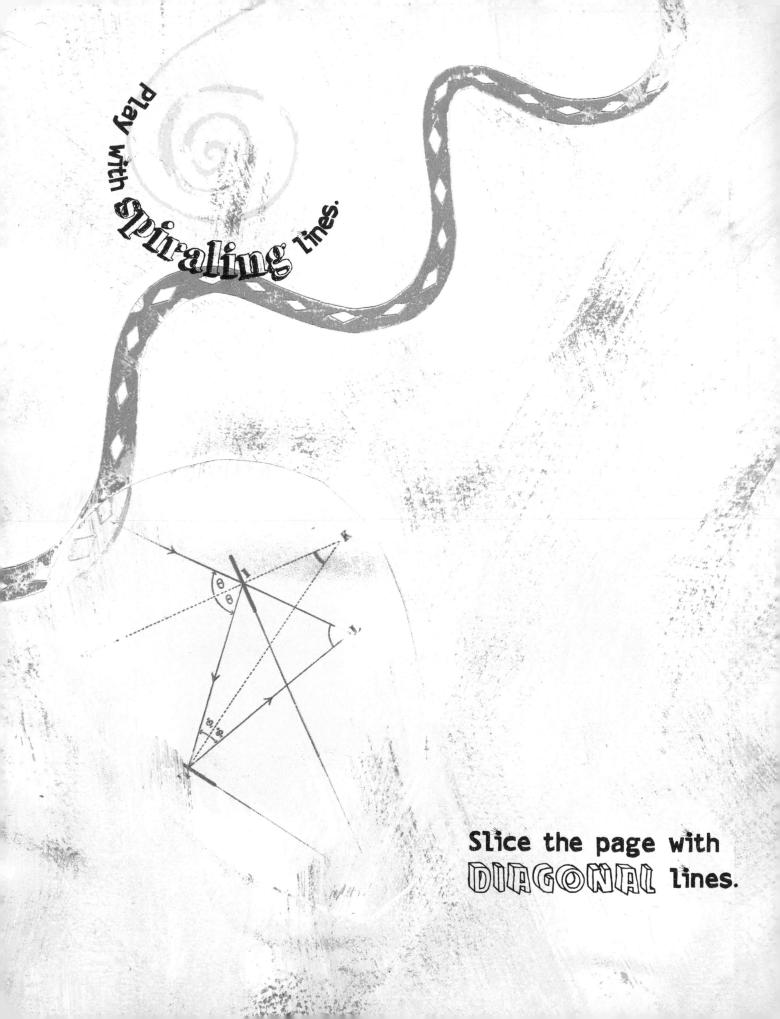

Play with **spiraling** lines.

Slice the page with
DIAGONAL lines.

Try drawing just *wavy* lines.

Experiment with
ZIGZAGGED lines.

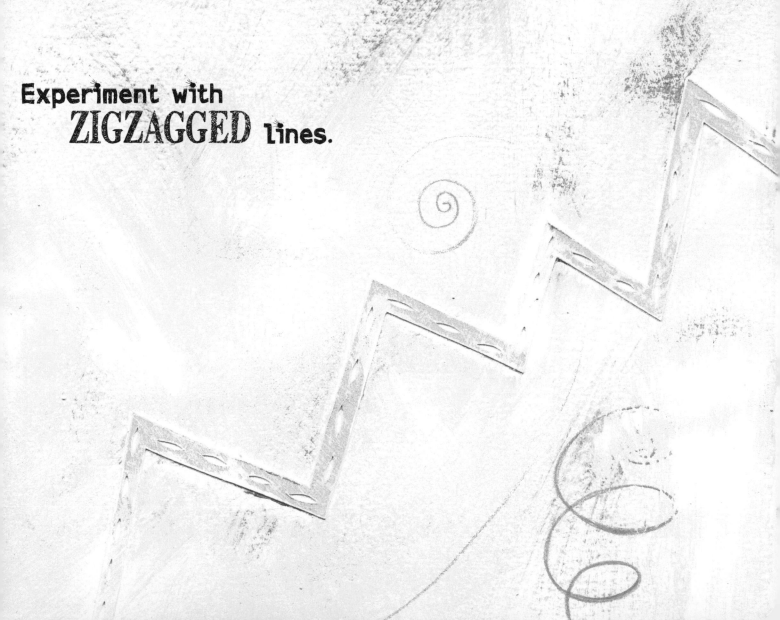

Fill these pages with bright and colorful
monsters to play with.

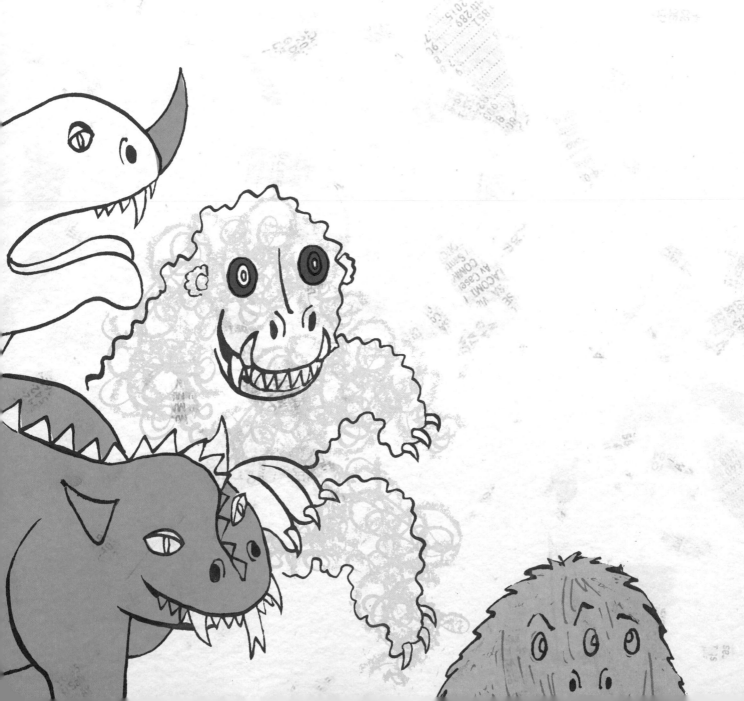

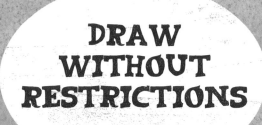

Pick a **color.**
　　　　Look around and draw what
you see of that color.

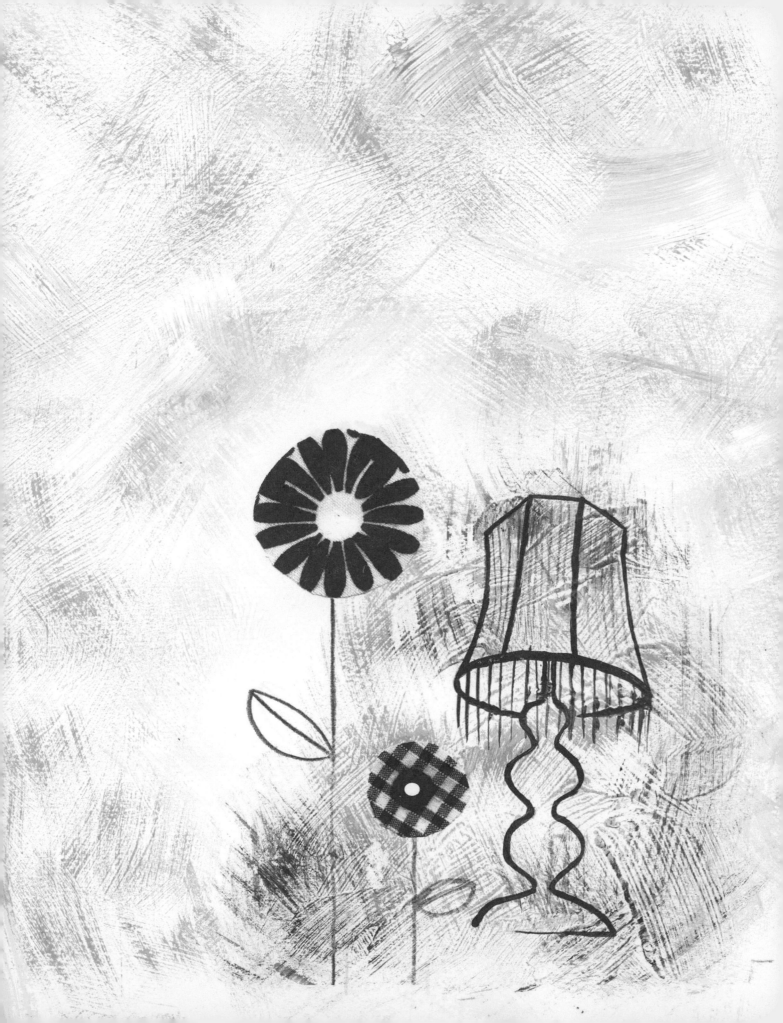

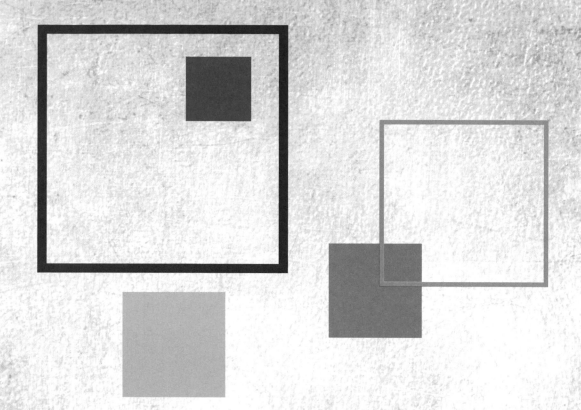

Fill this page with

squares.

Can you turn those squares into
robots and
machines?

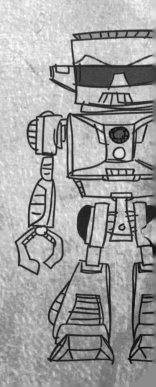

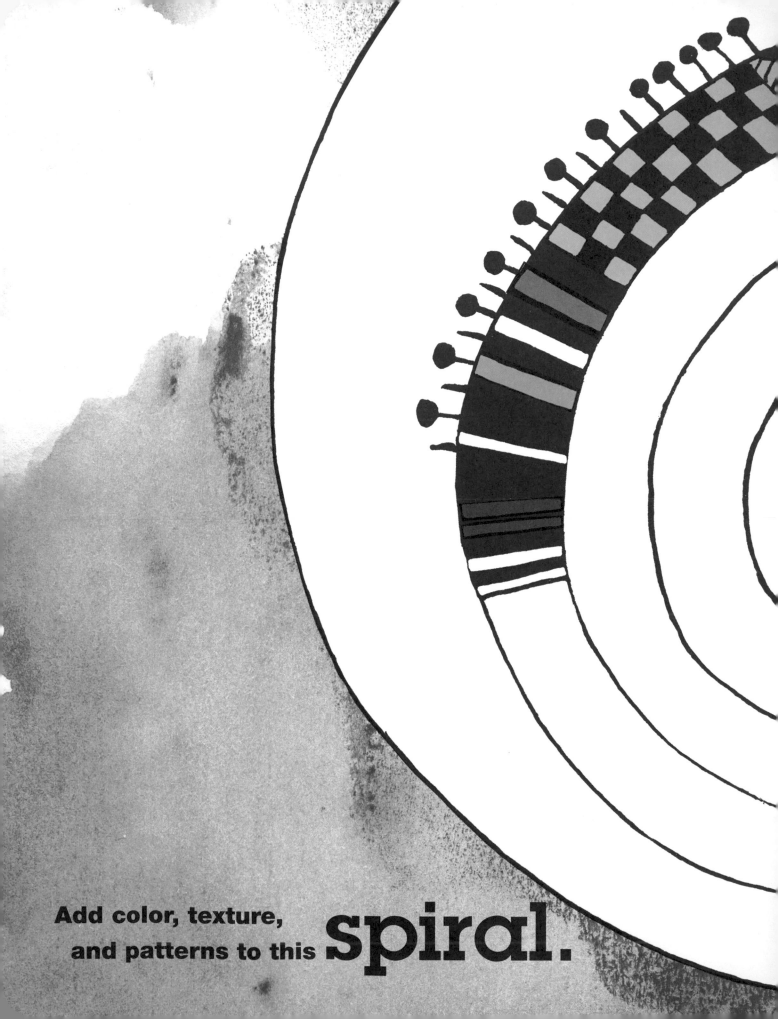

Add color, texture, and patterns to this spiral.

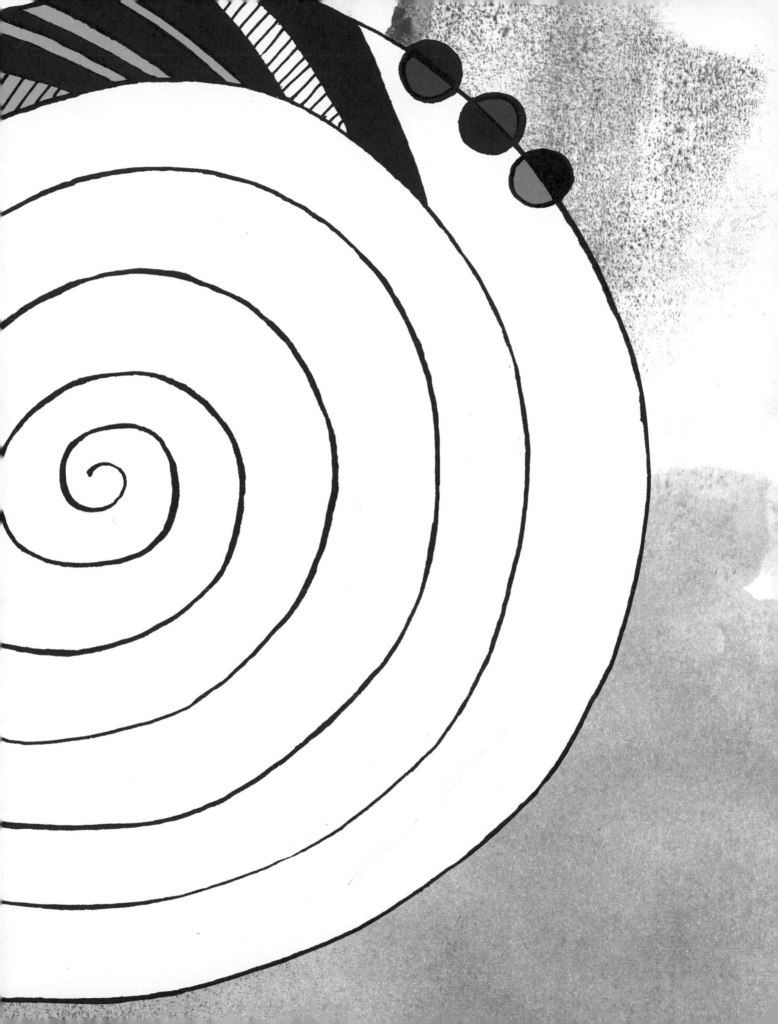

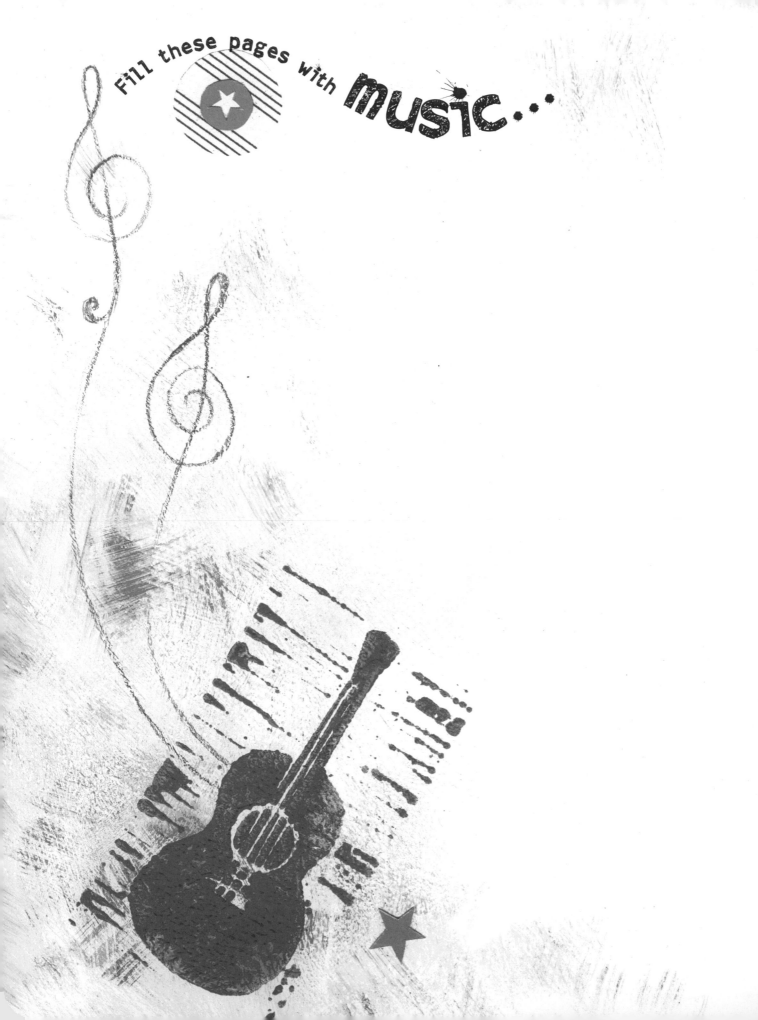

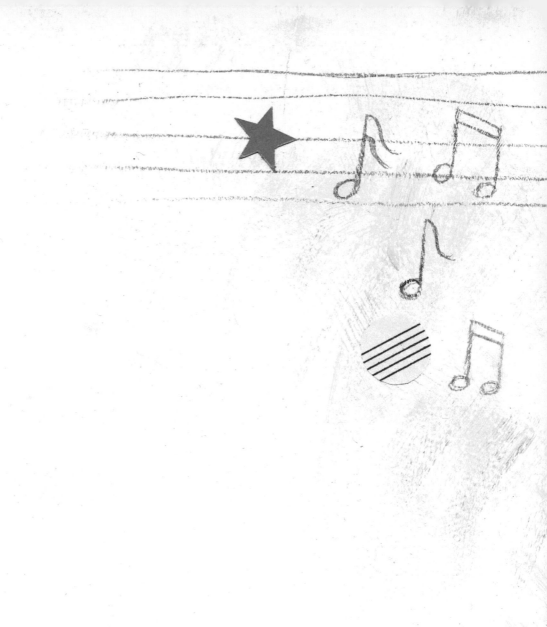

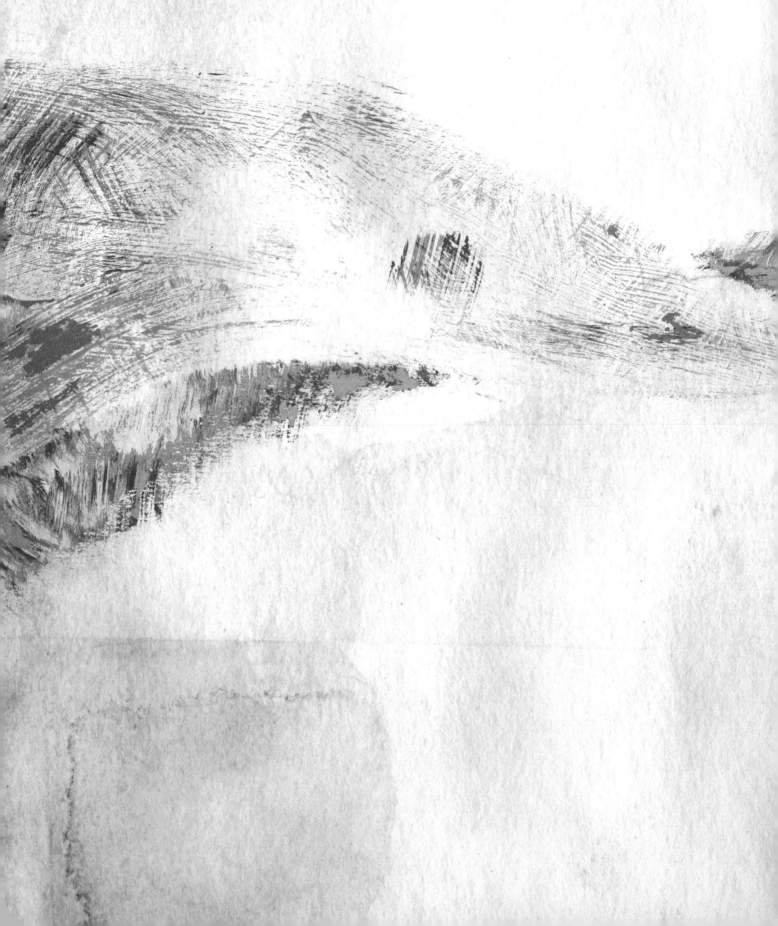

Don't think, just draw.

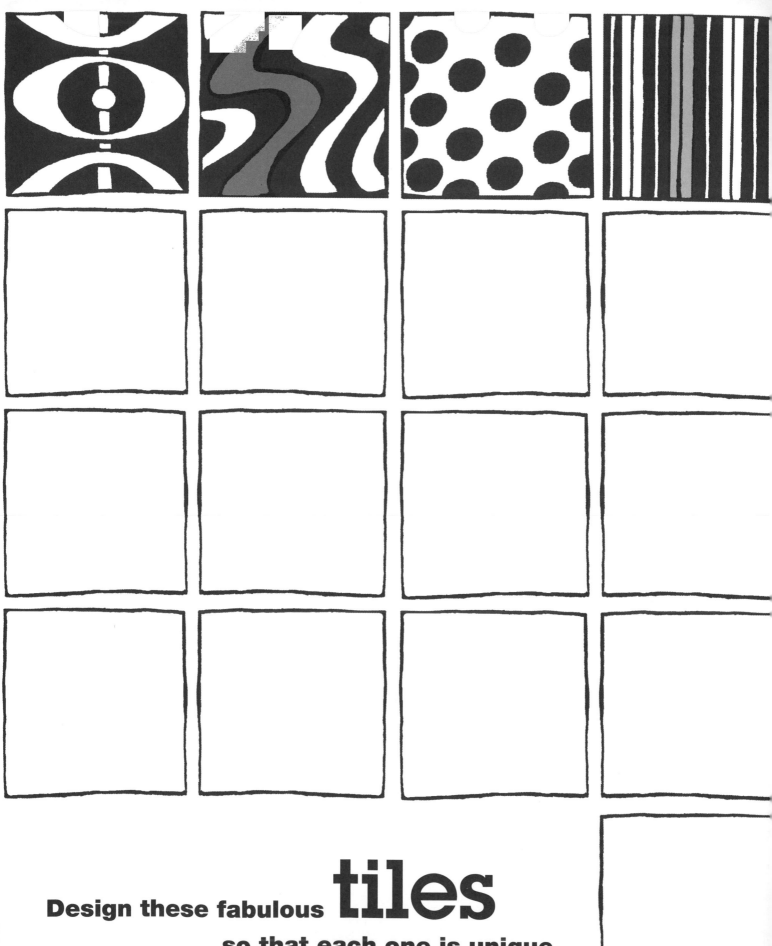

Design these fabulous tiles
so that each one is unique.

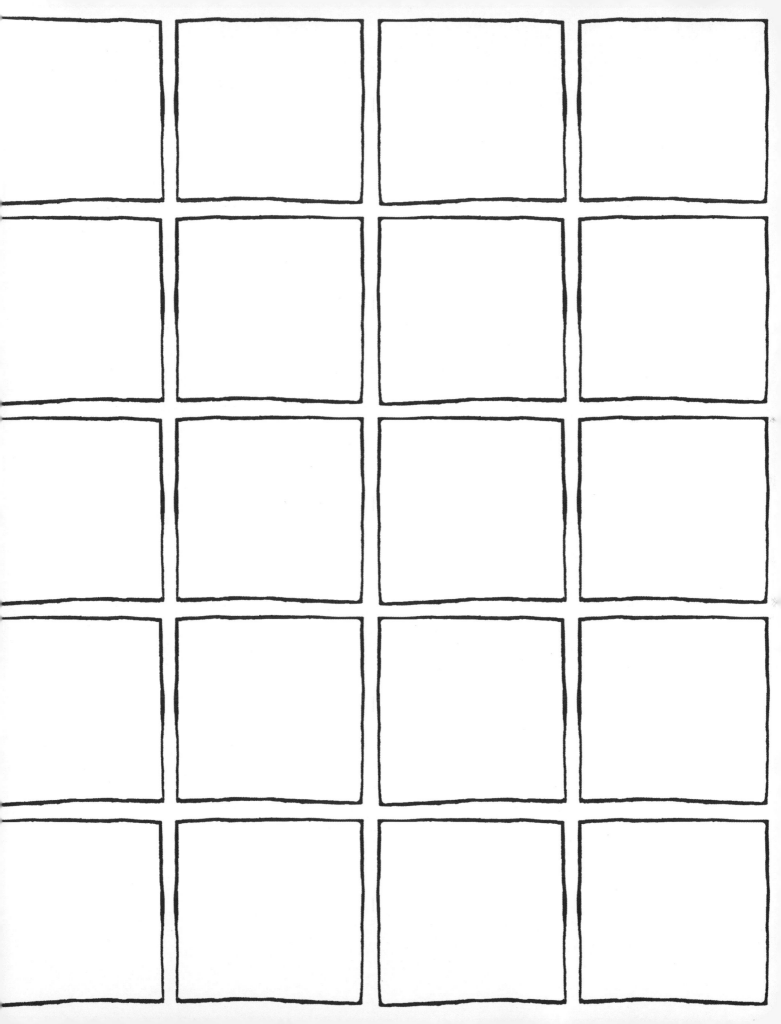

Using a single line draw a SKYLINE.

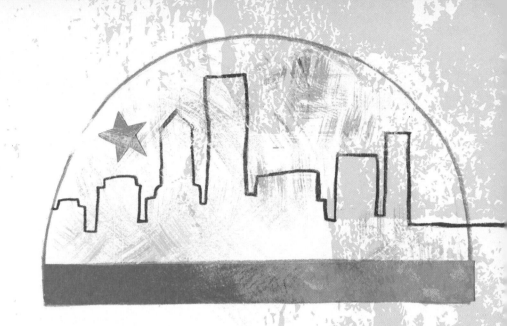

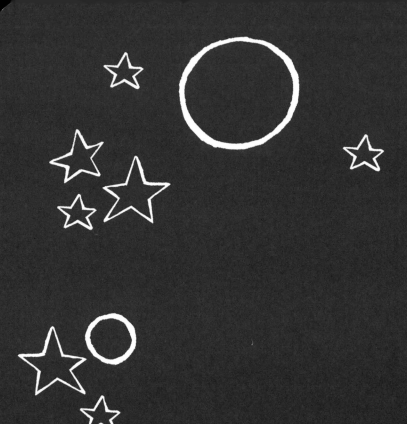

Draw a **rocket**
flying to the moon.

"I PAINT OBJECTS AS I THINK THEM, NOT AS I SEE THEM."

Pablo Picasso.

Draw different shapes from your imagination.

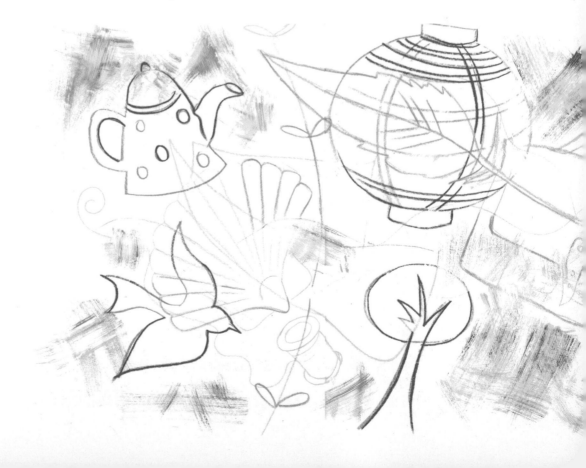

Use the **gridlines** to guide your doodles.

Draw something that begins with the letter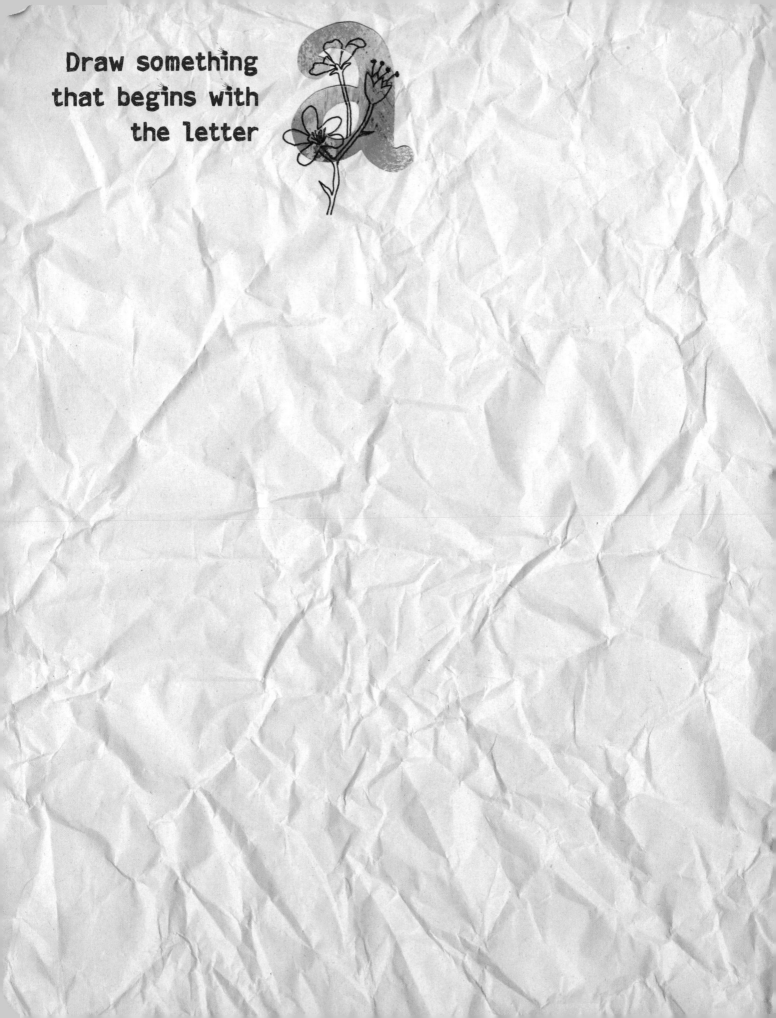

Draw something that begins with the letter

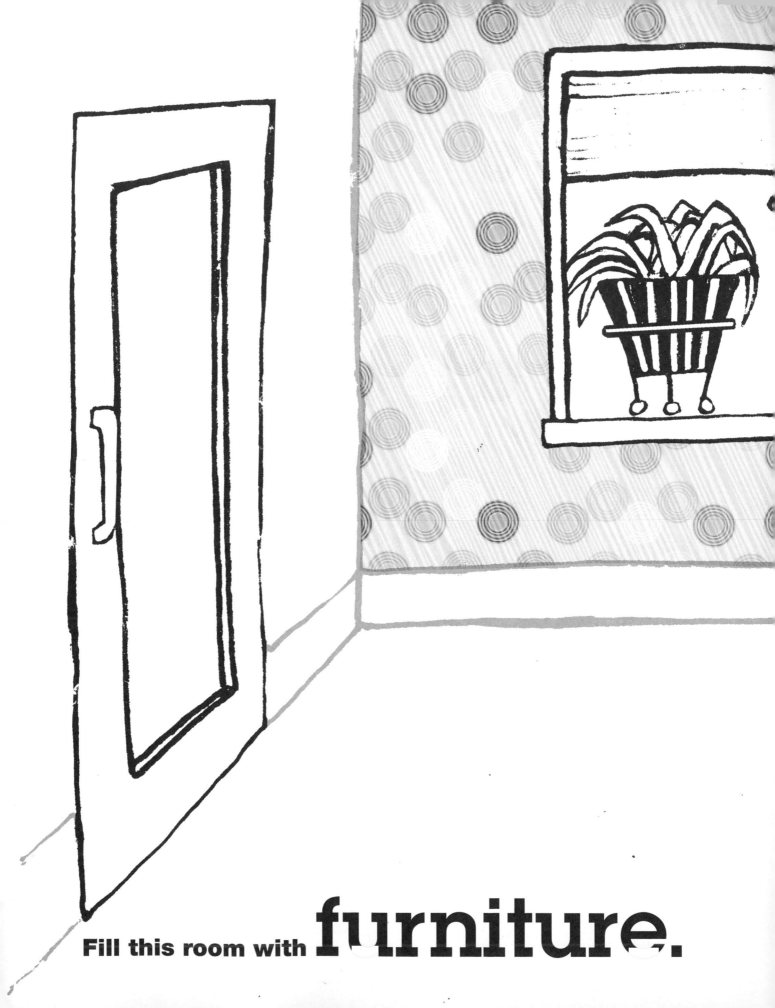

Fill this room with furniture.

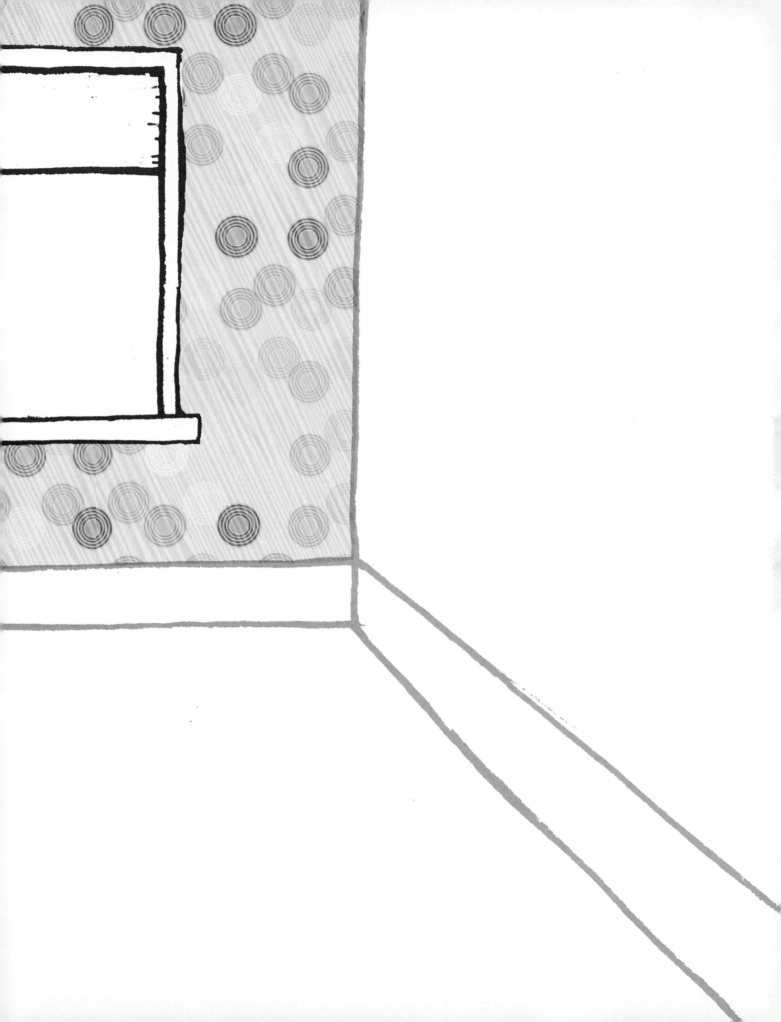

Fill these pages with

birds in flight.

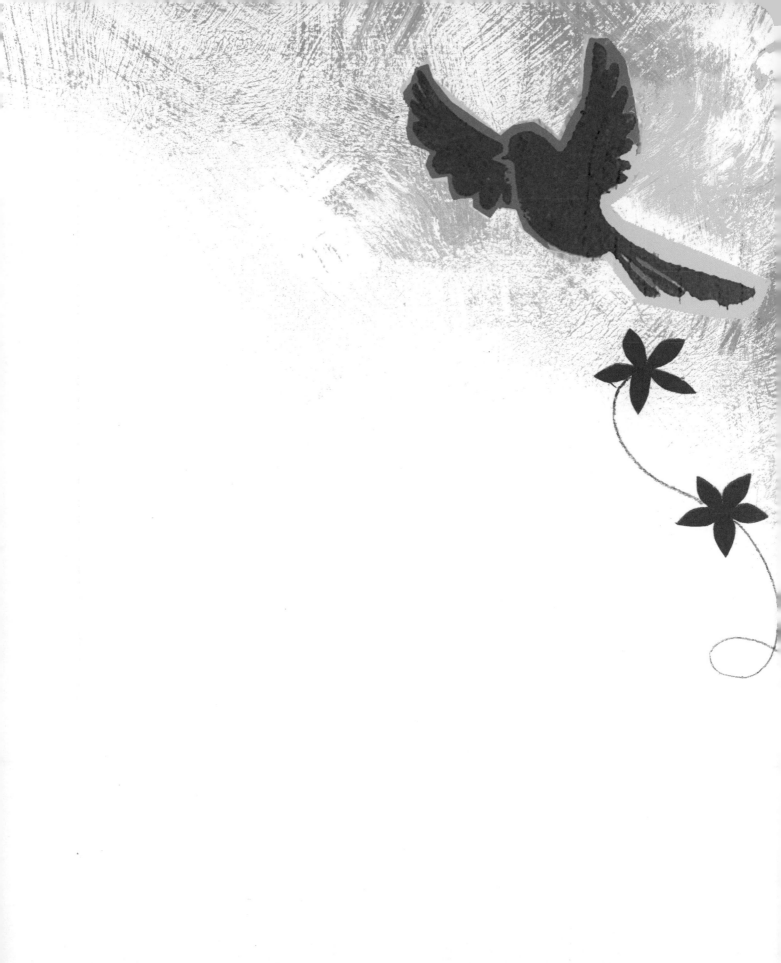

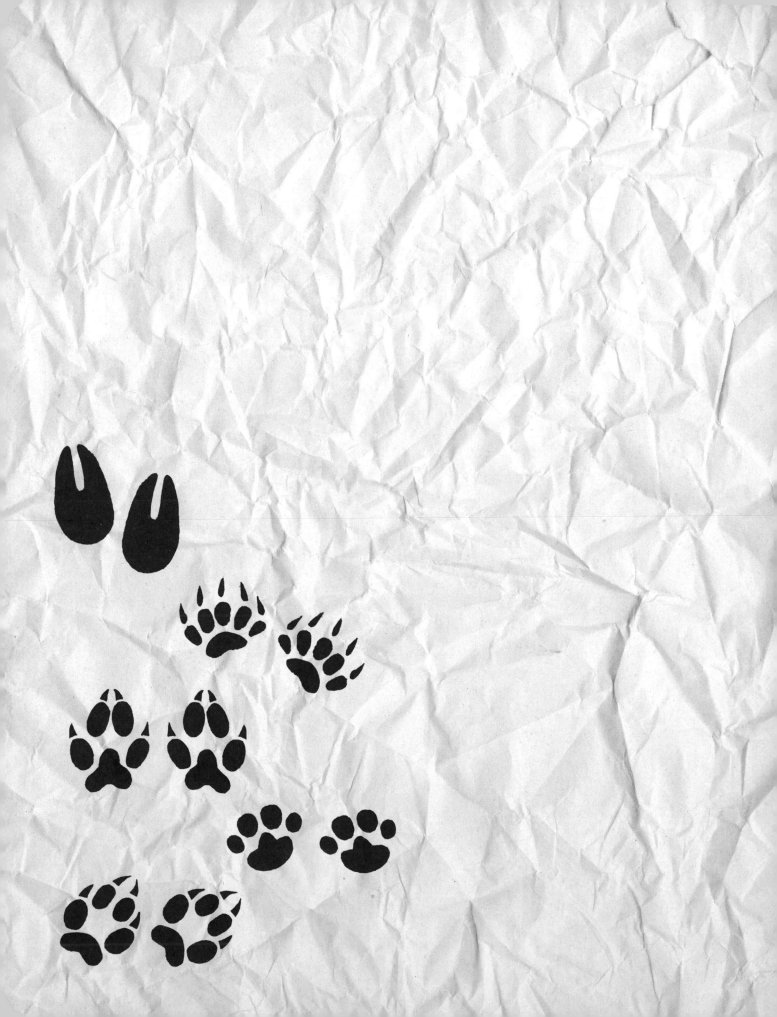

Fill these pages with different
animal footprints.

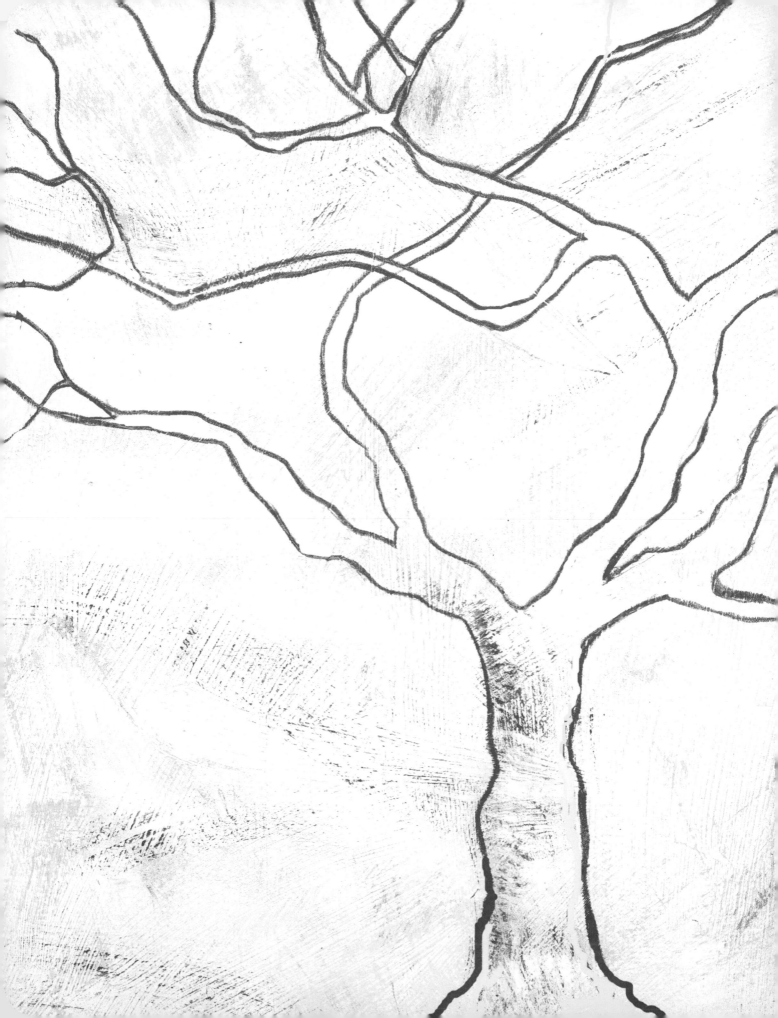

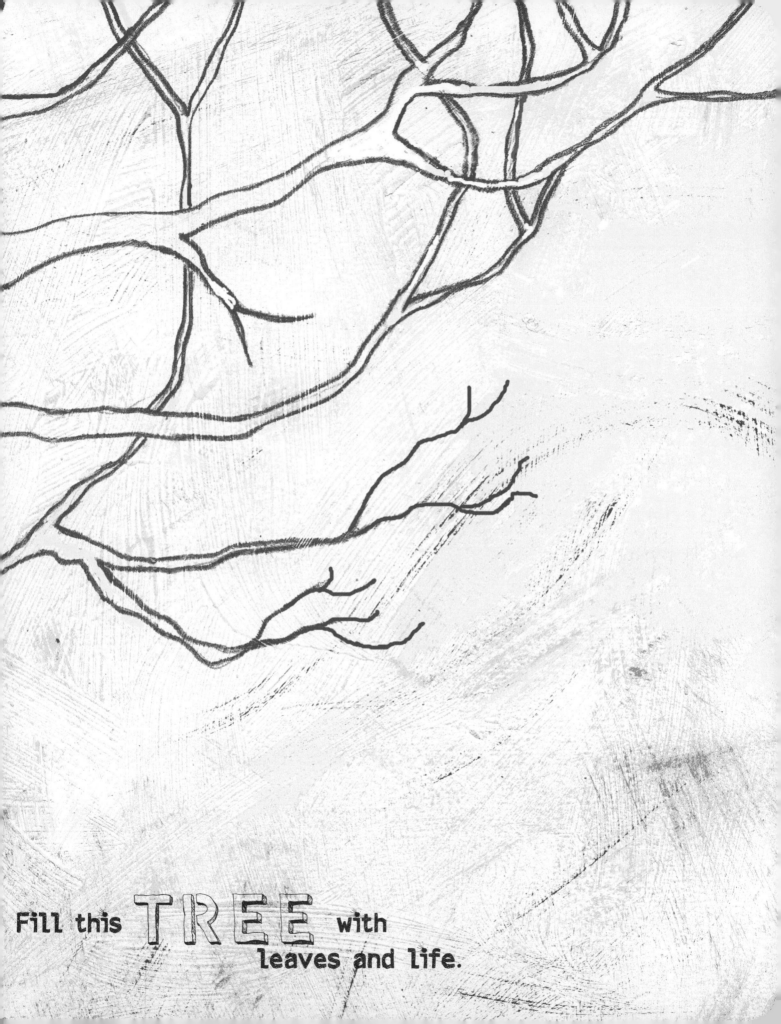

Fill this TREE with leaves and life.

Fill these jars with your favorite
candies and cookies.

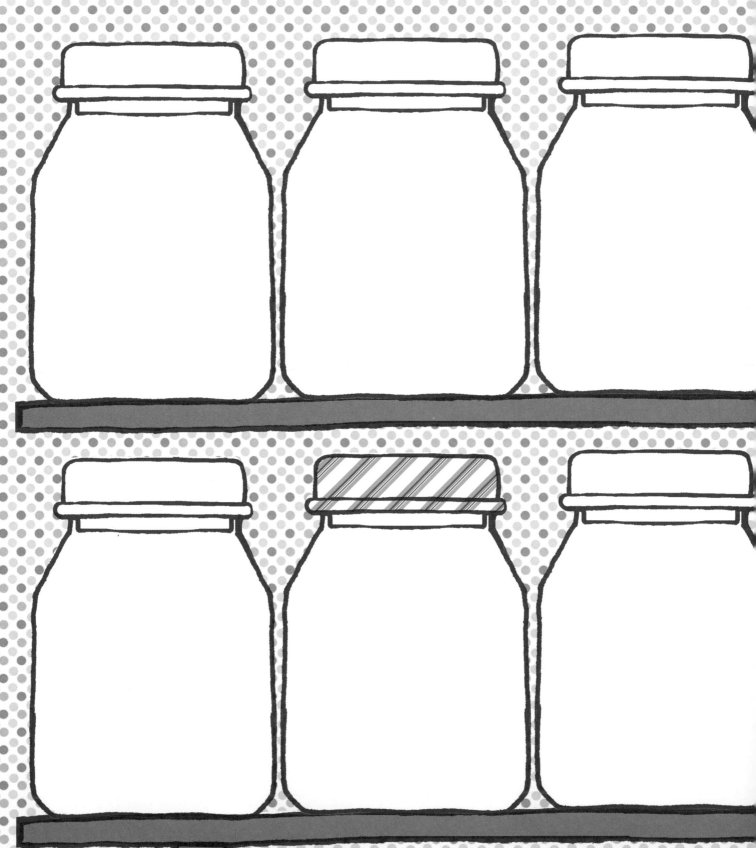

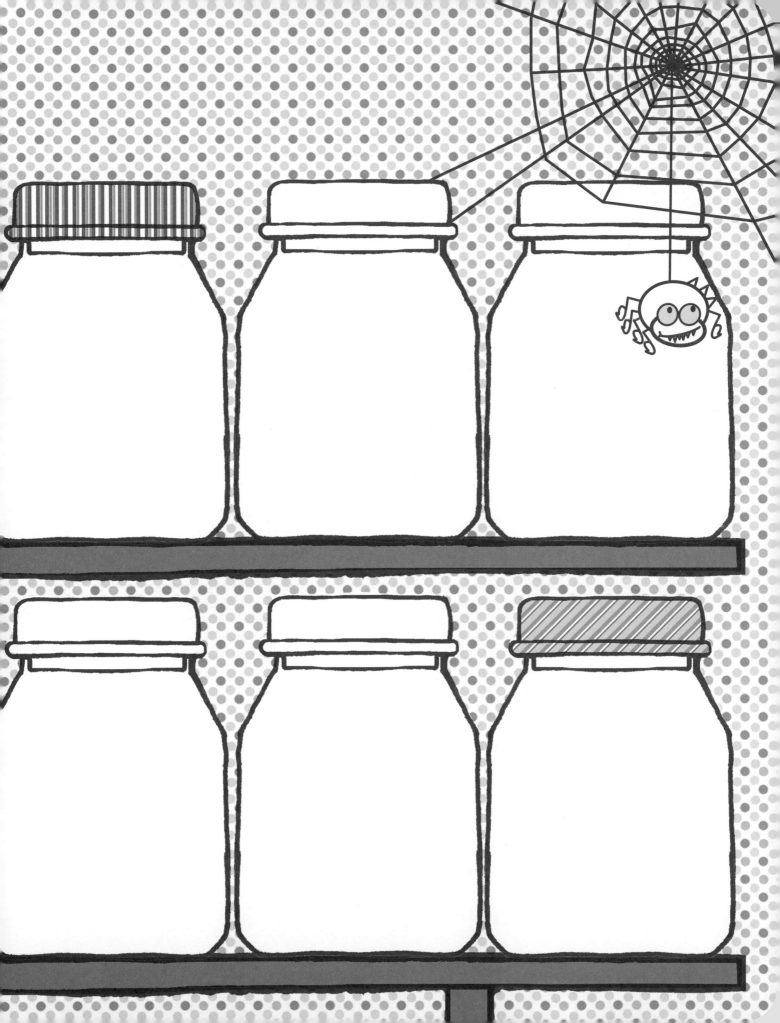

Draw some monsters.

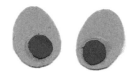

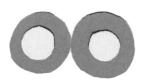

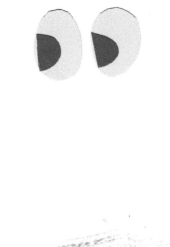

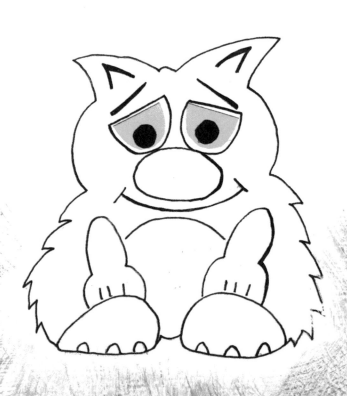

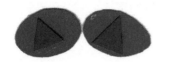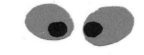

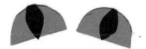

There are no limits.

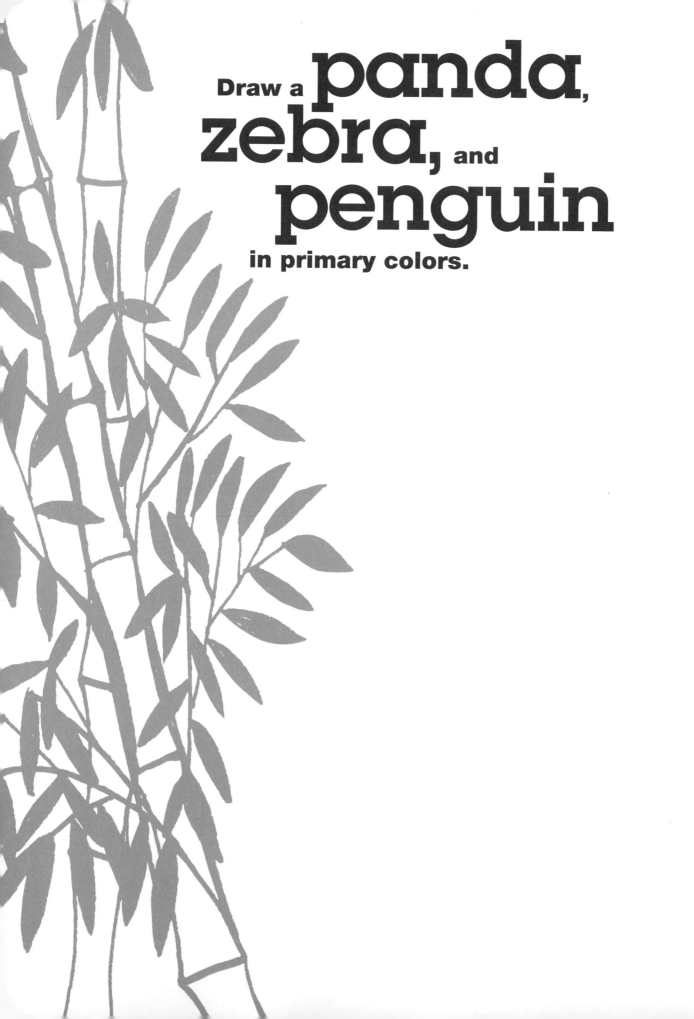

Draw a **panda,** **zebra,** and **penguin**

in primary colors.

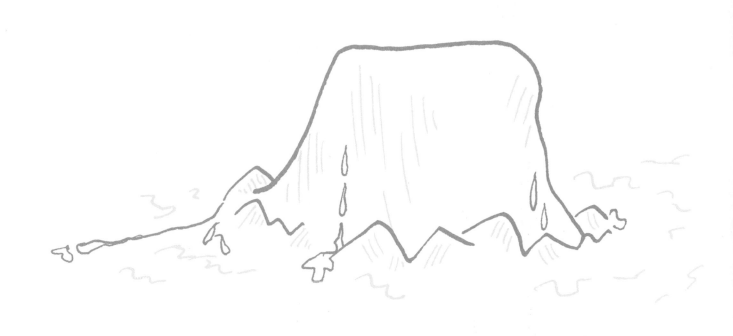

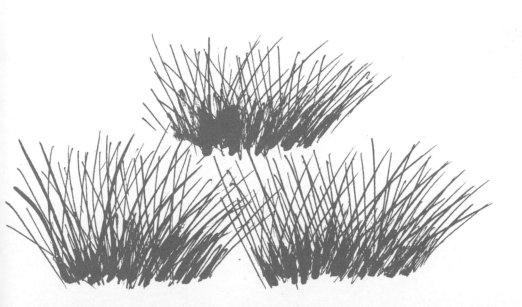

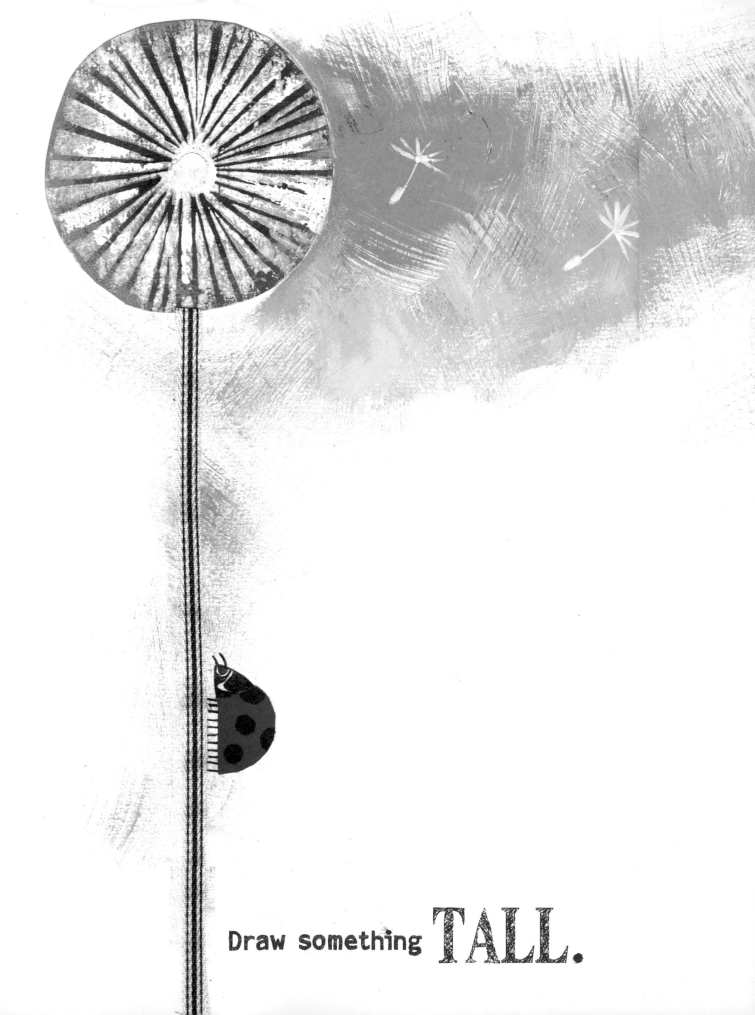

Draw something TALL.

Draw something *small*.

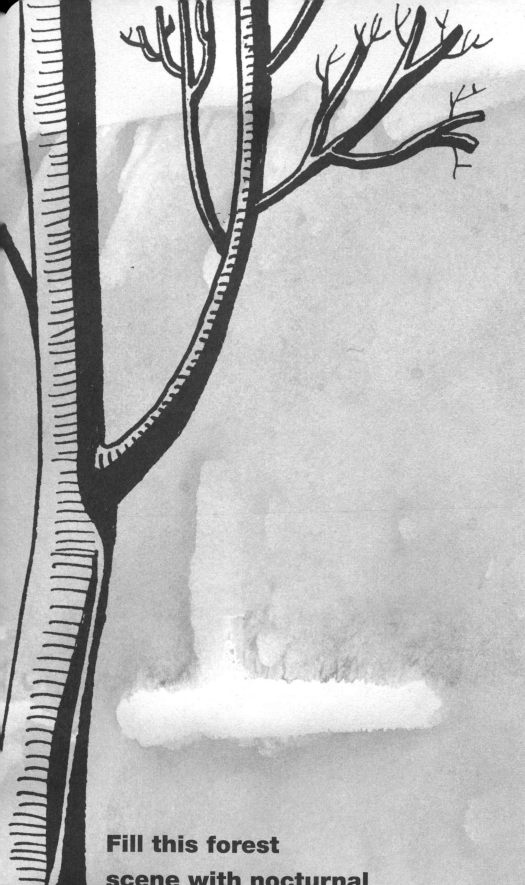

**Fill this forest
scene with nocturnal
animals.**

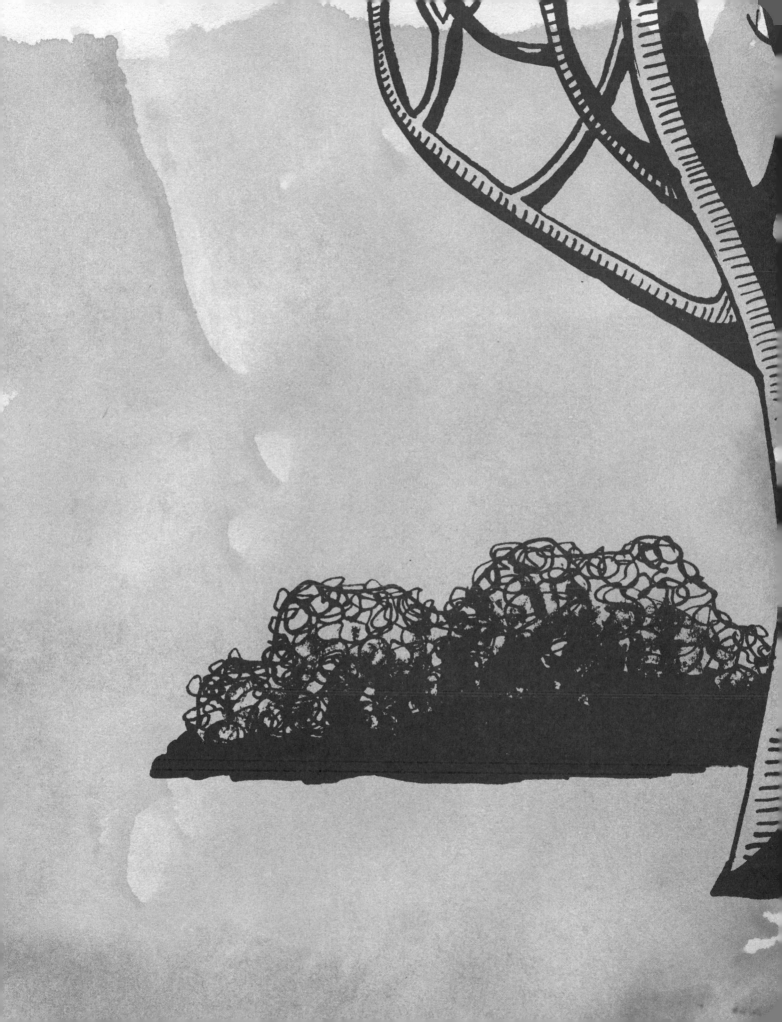

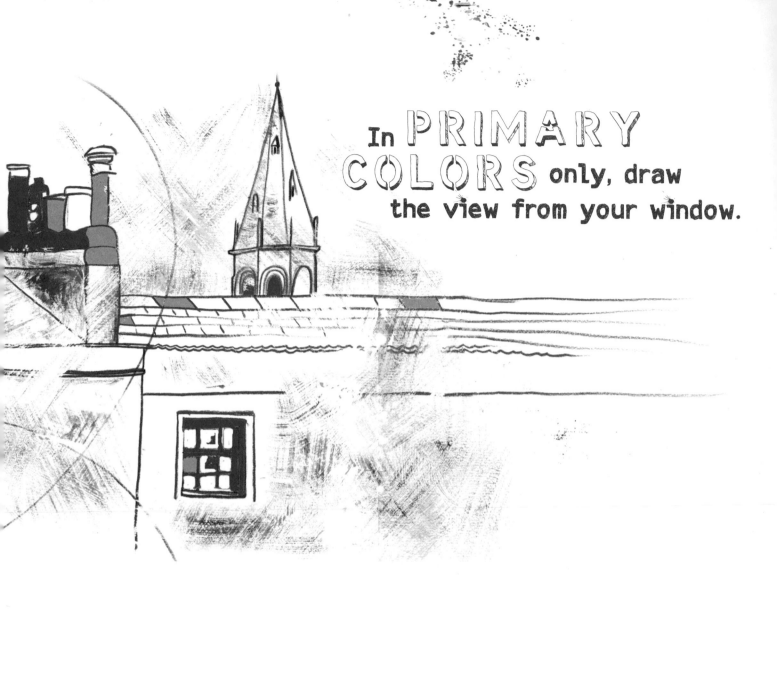

In **PRIMARY COLORS** only, draw the view from your window.

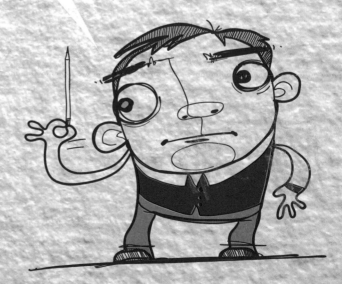

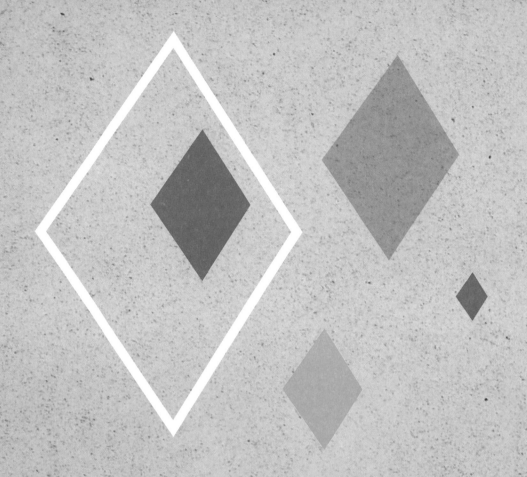

Fill this page with diamonds.

Can you turn those diamonds into something alive?

Draw a **night sky.**

Plant a flower garden on these pages.

Draw the last thing you read.

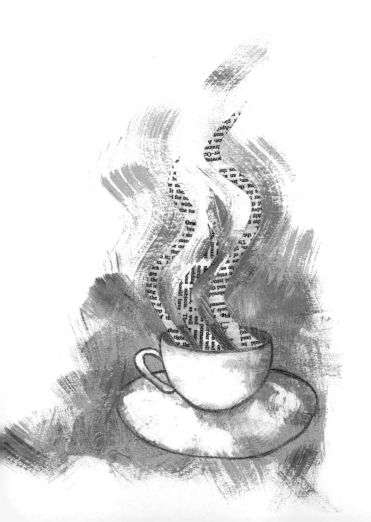

"You can't depend on your eyes when your imagination is out of focus."

Mark Twain.

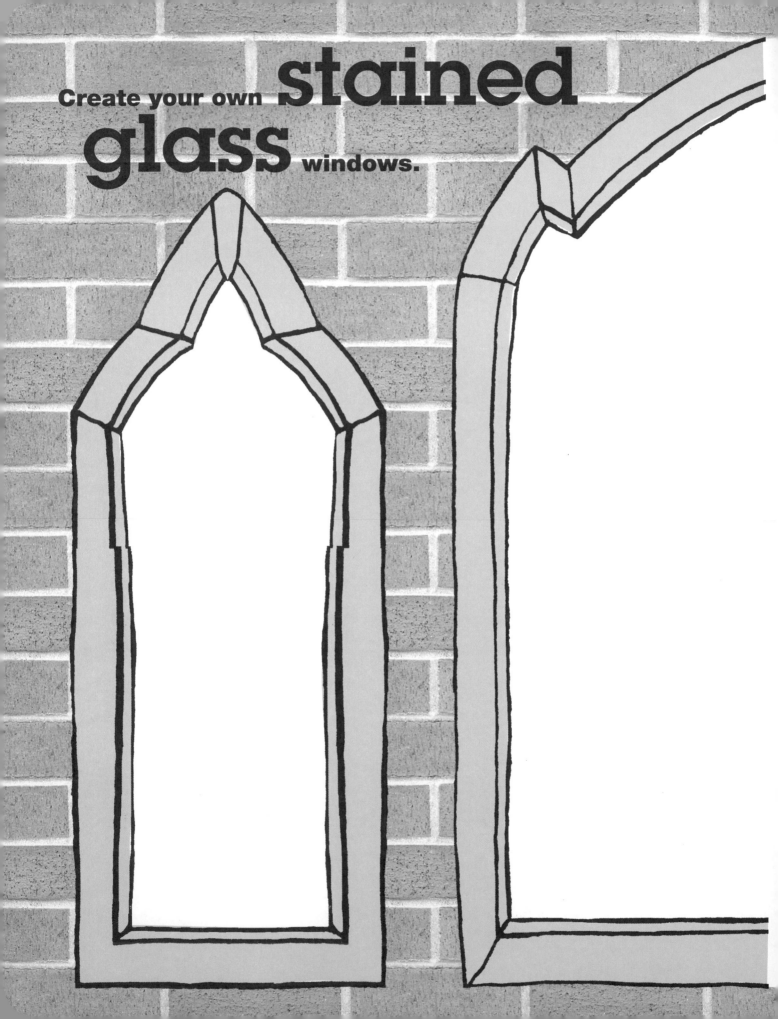

Create your own **stained glass** windows.

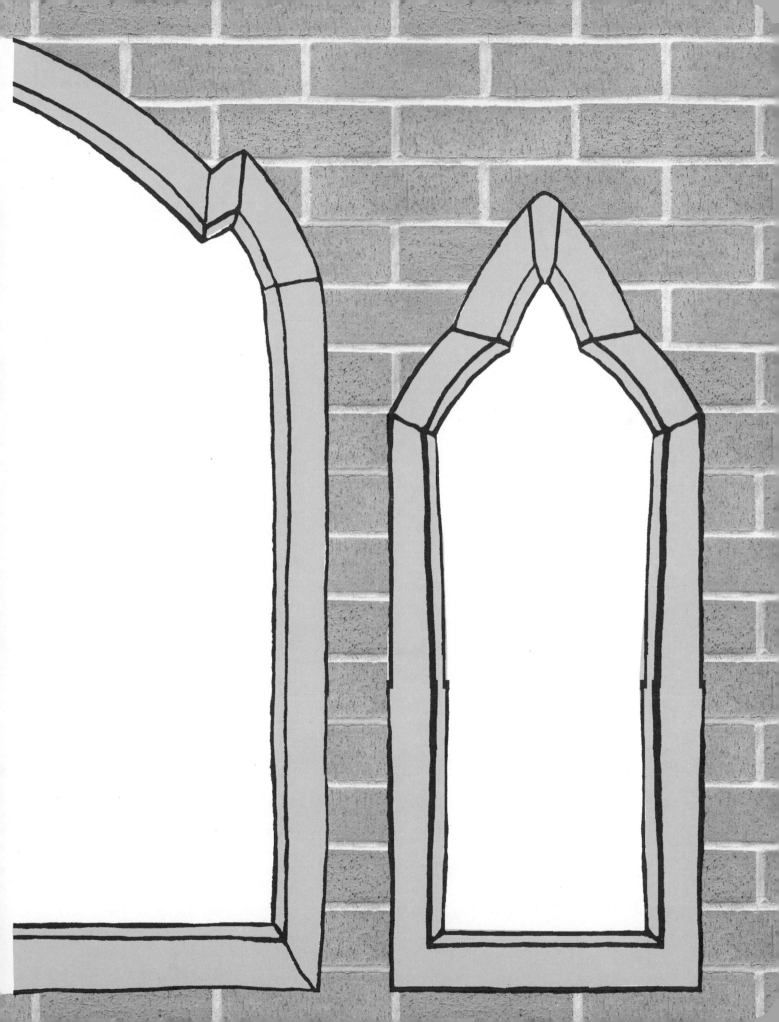

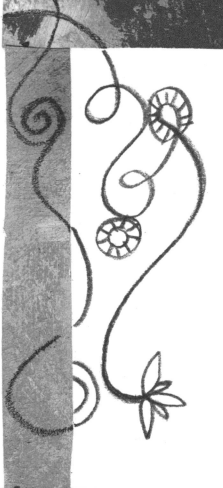

Fill these
pages with **doodles...**
can you do it without taking your
pencil off the page?

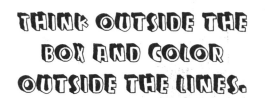

THINK OUTSIDE THE BOX AND COLOR OUTSIDE THE LINES.

Finish this cityscape.

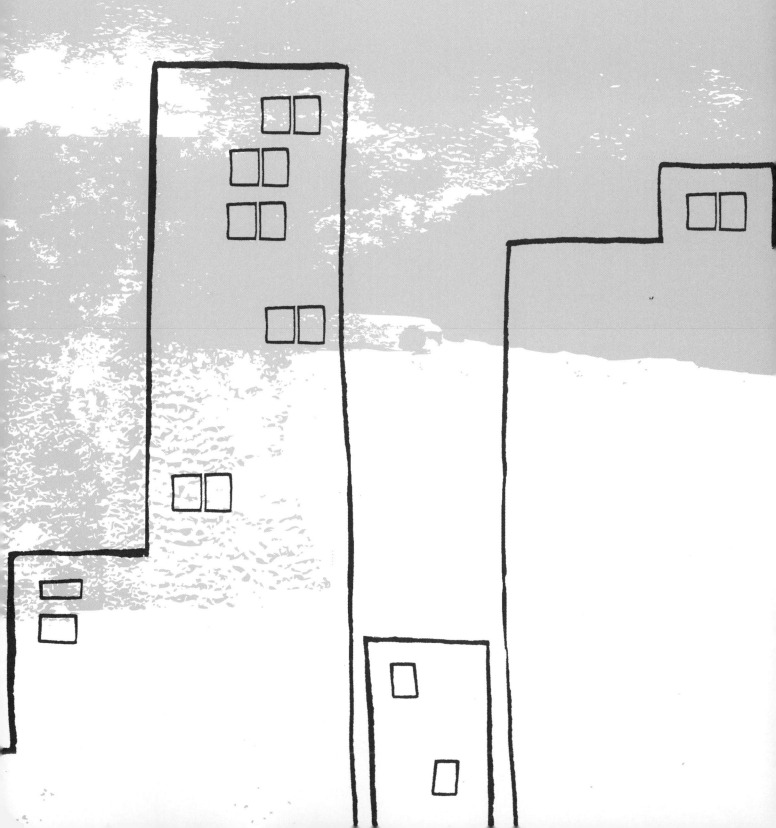

Draw some automobiles on this street.

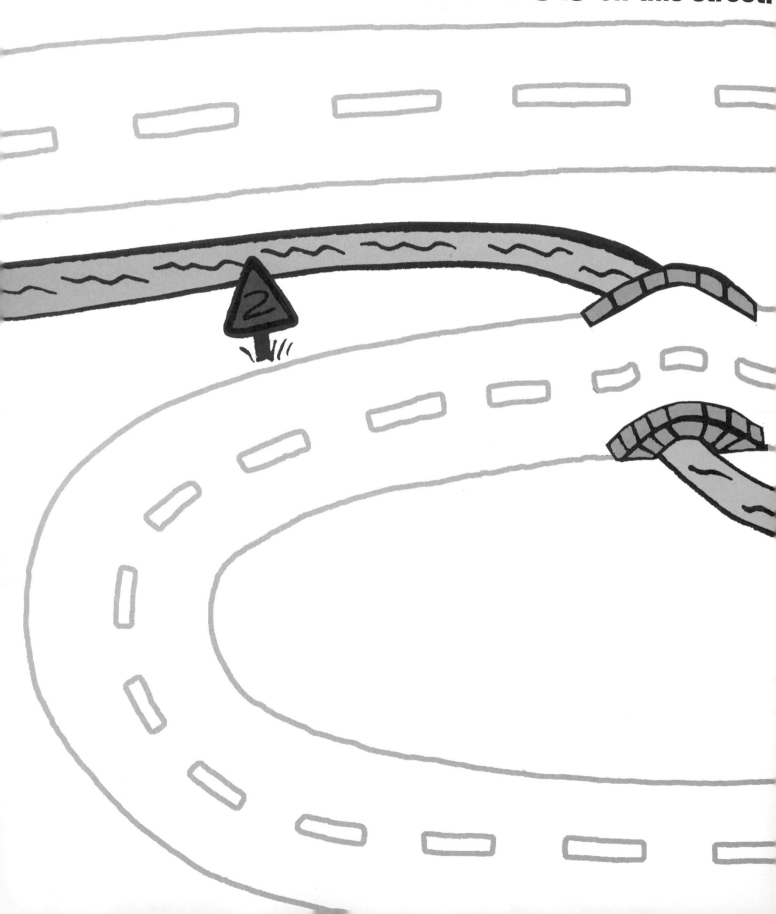

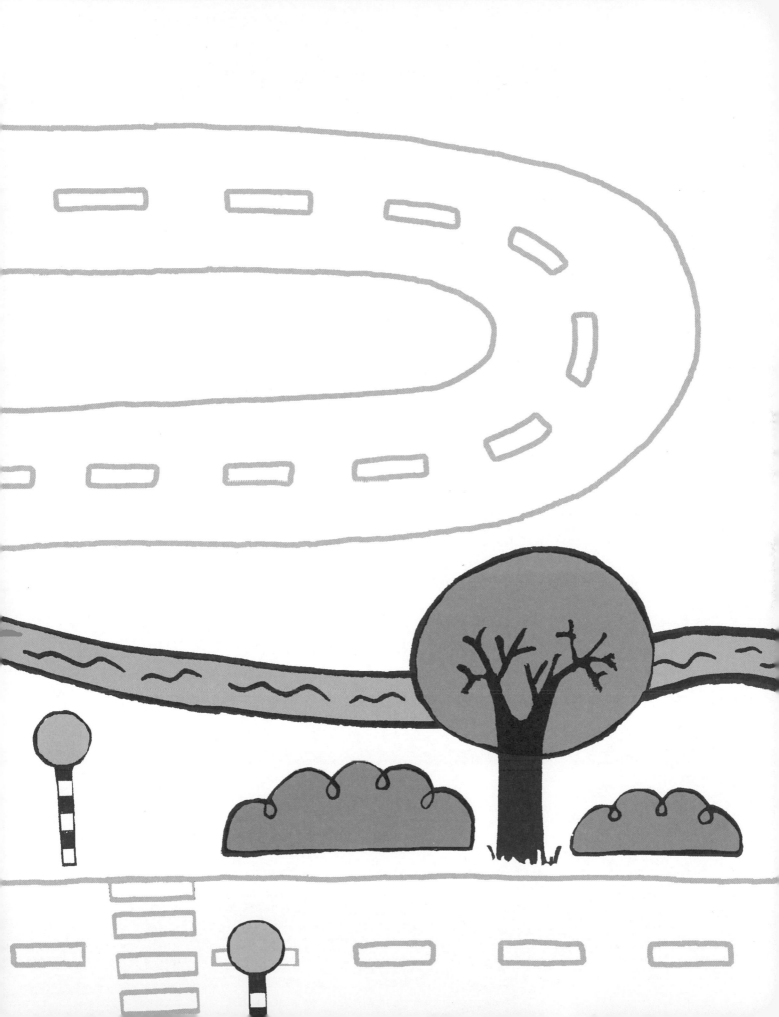

Draw a self-portrait using only **ZIGZAGGED** lines.

Add personalities to the
people in this crowd.

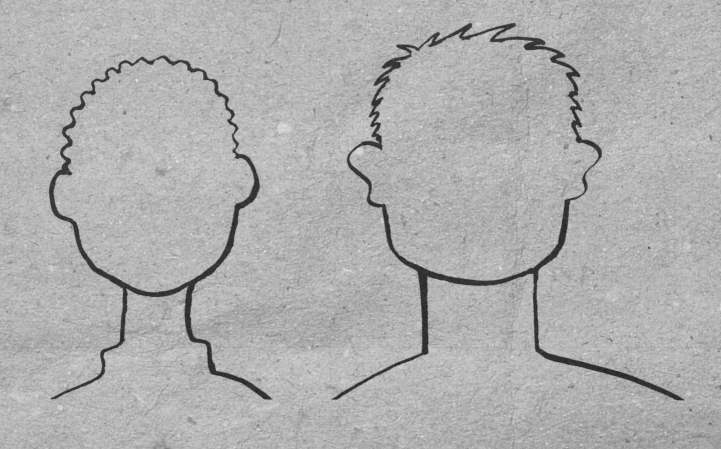

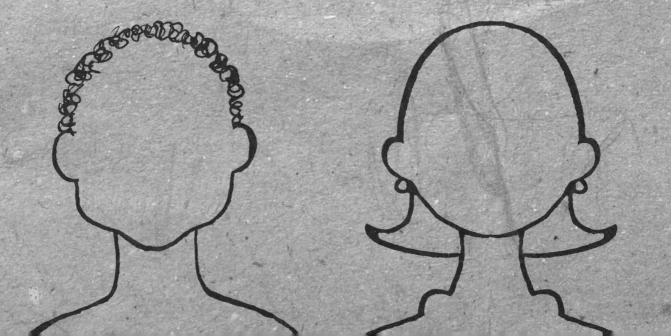

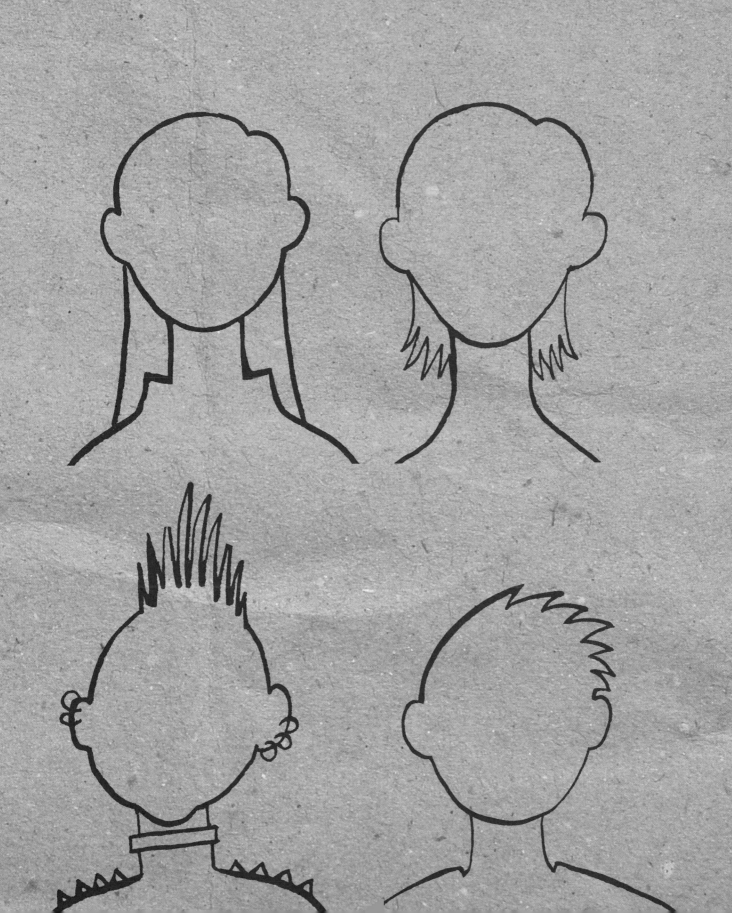

"There are no only areas against

lines in nature, of color, one another." Edouard Manet.

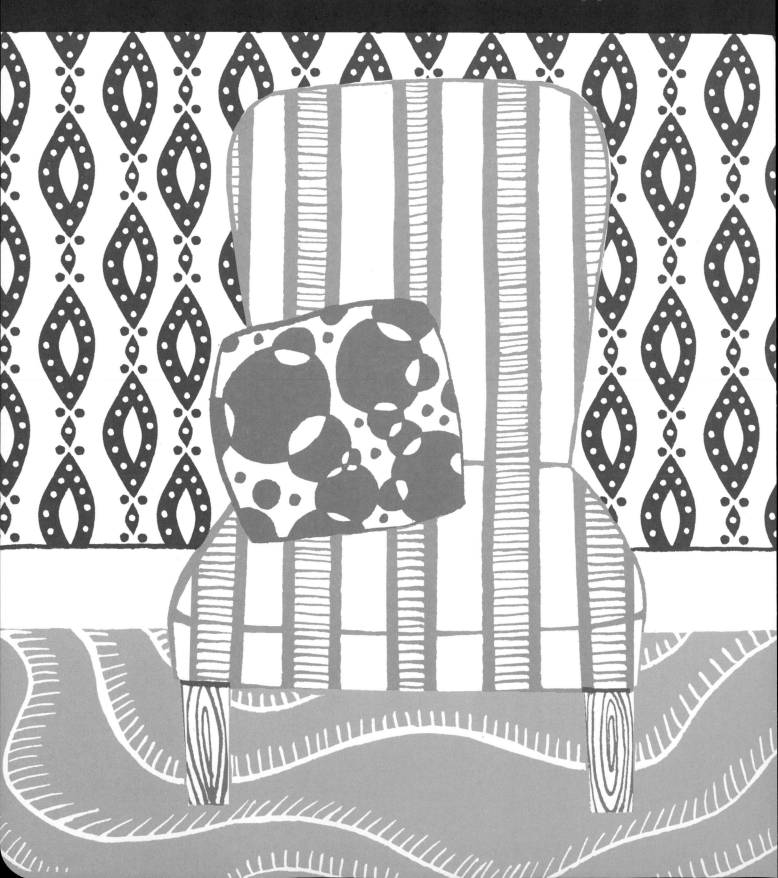

Draw a *thunderstorm.*

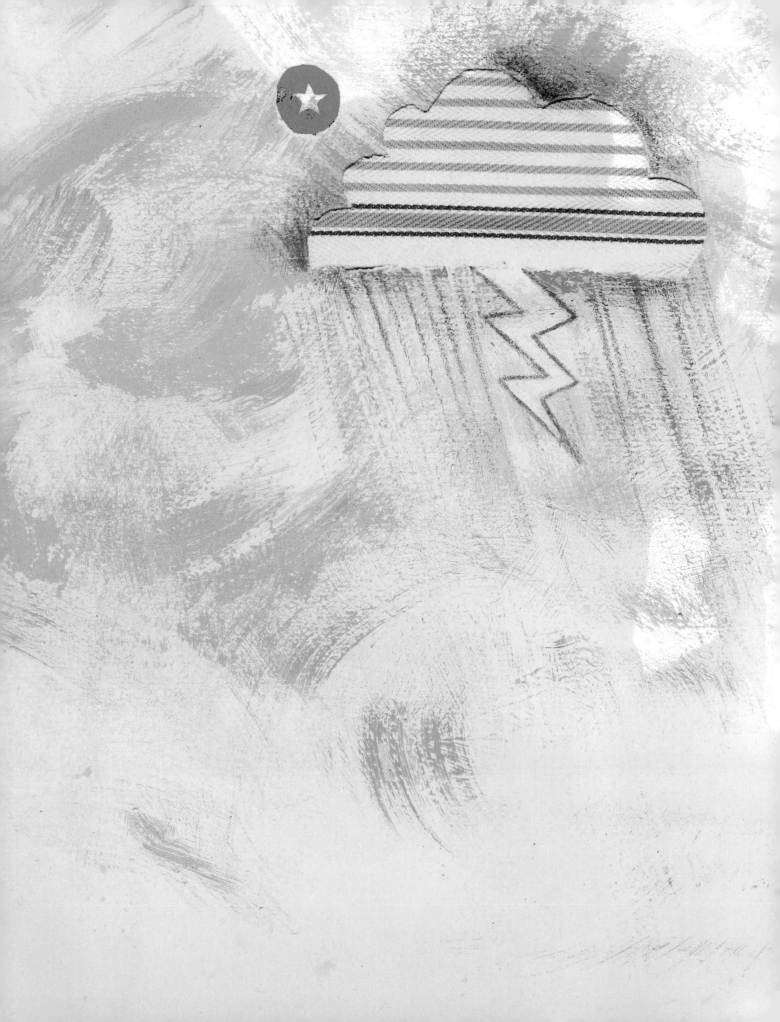

Fill this jar with

jelly beans.

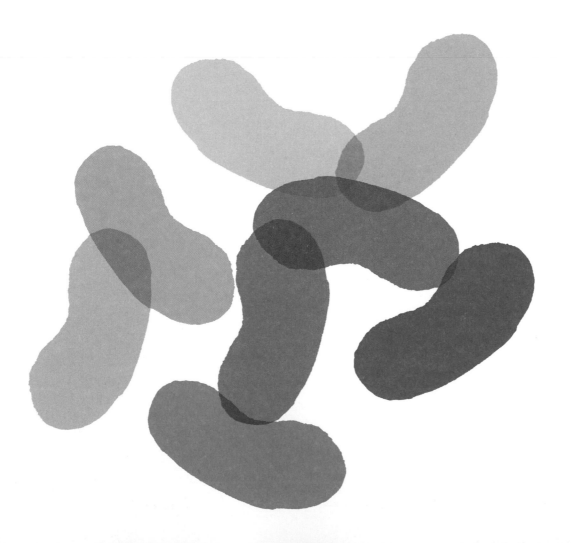

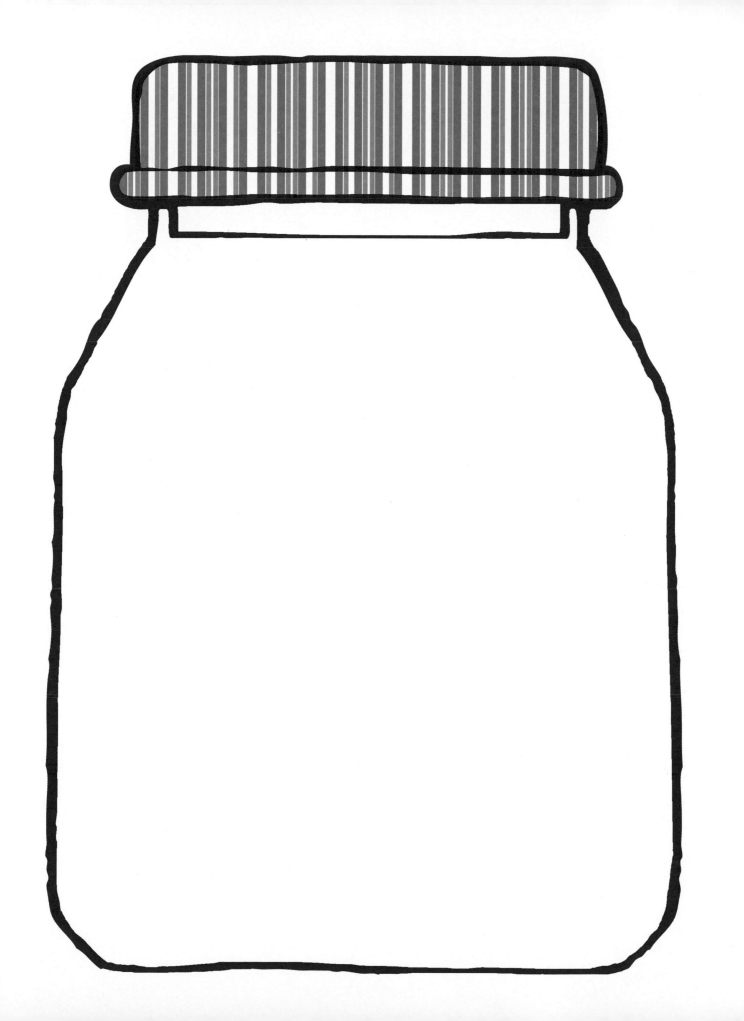

Draw something **furry.**

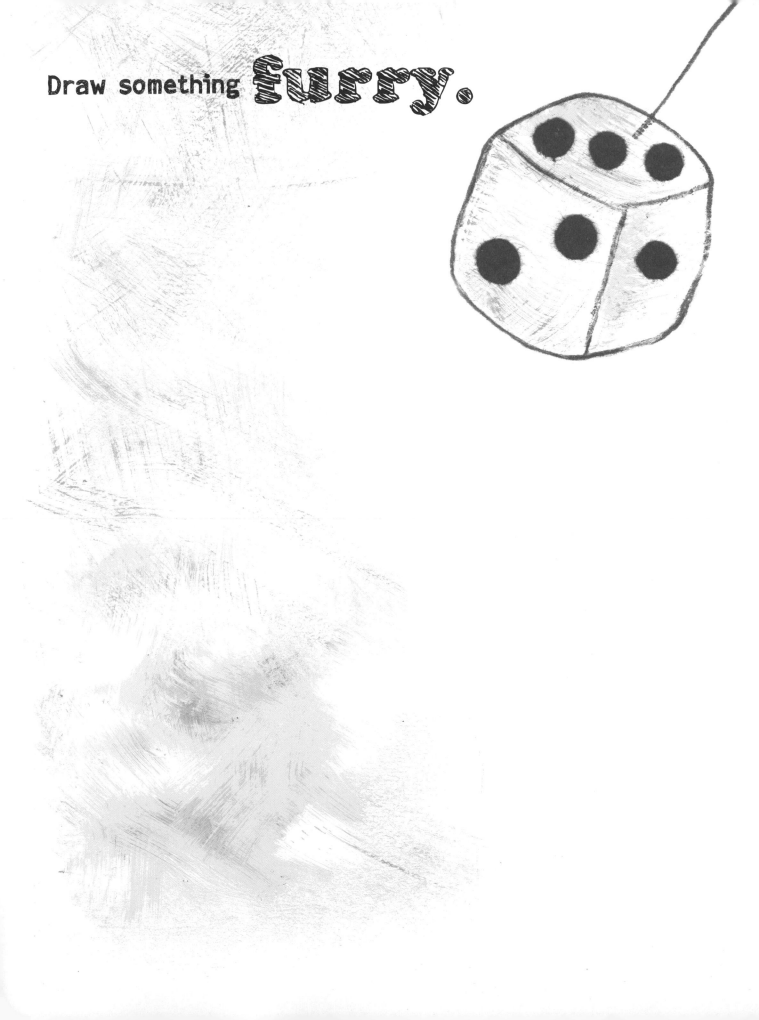

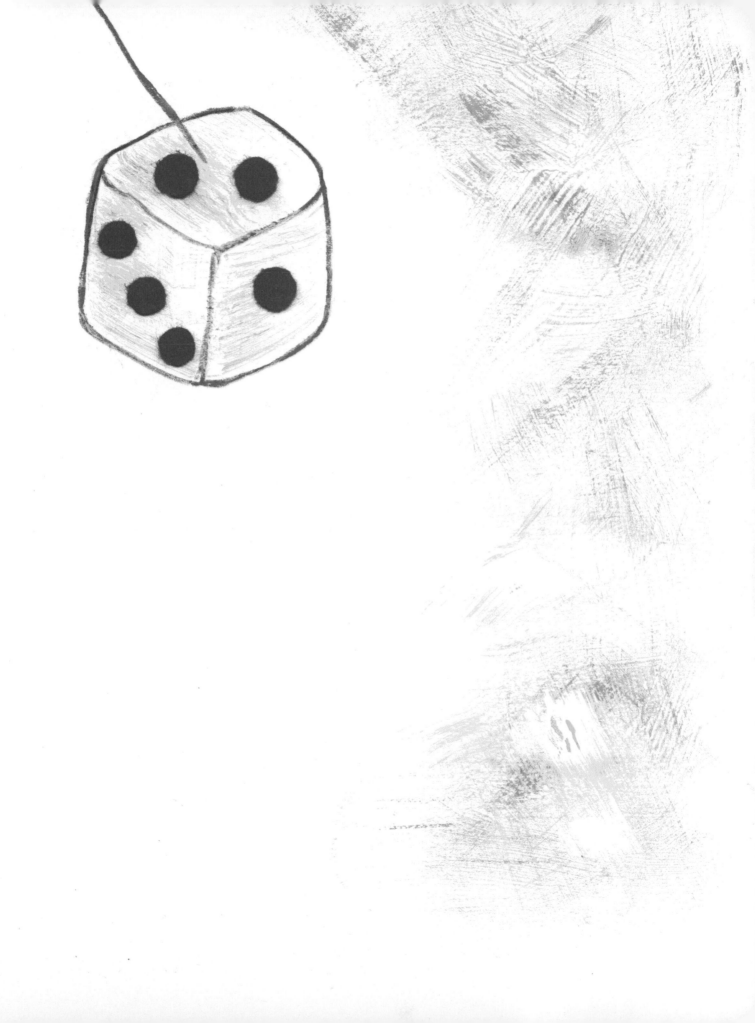

Fill this page with **stars.**

**Can you change those
stars into patterns?**

Draw an animal
using only spiraling lines.

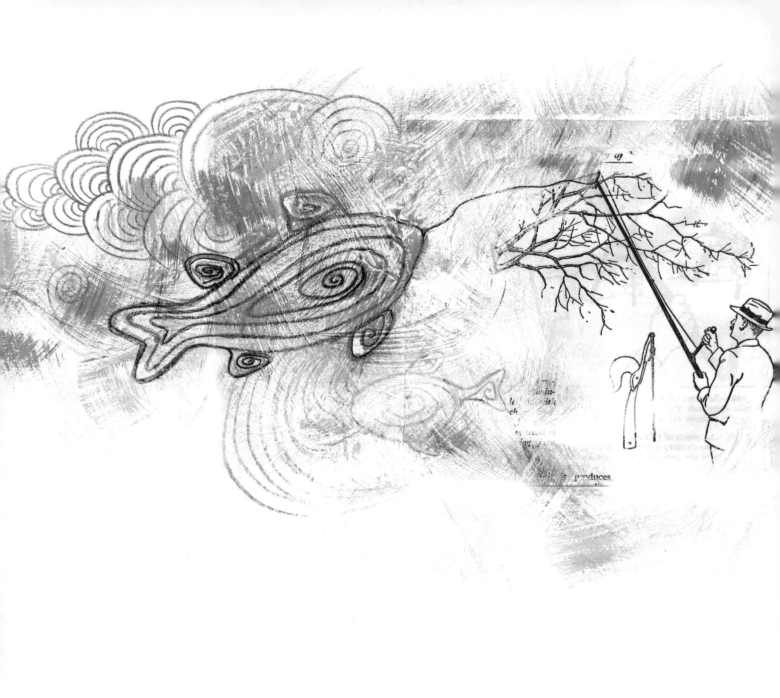

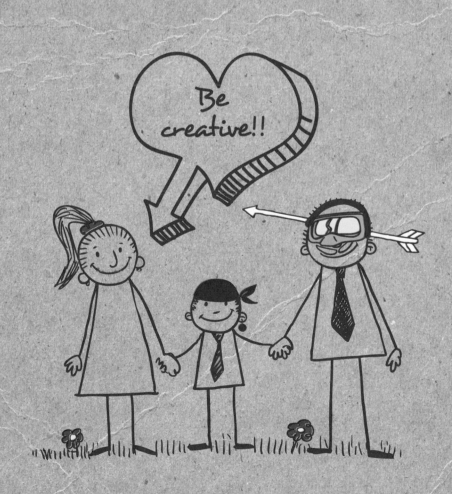

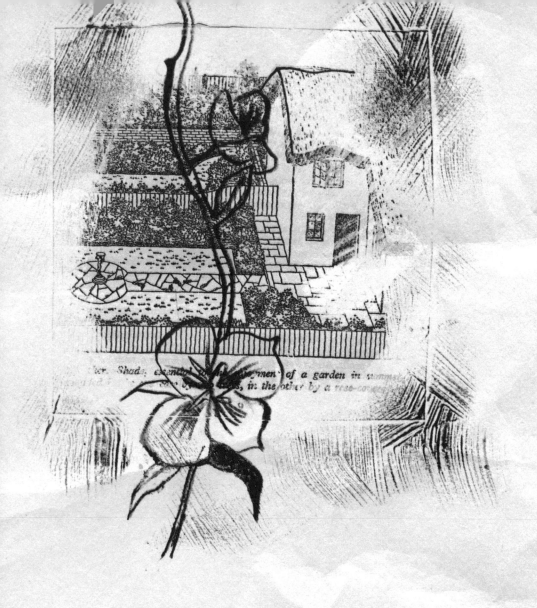

Using black tones only,
draw a **FLOWER GARDEN.**

Color these party hats.

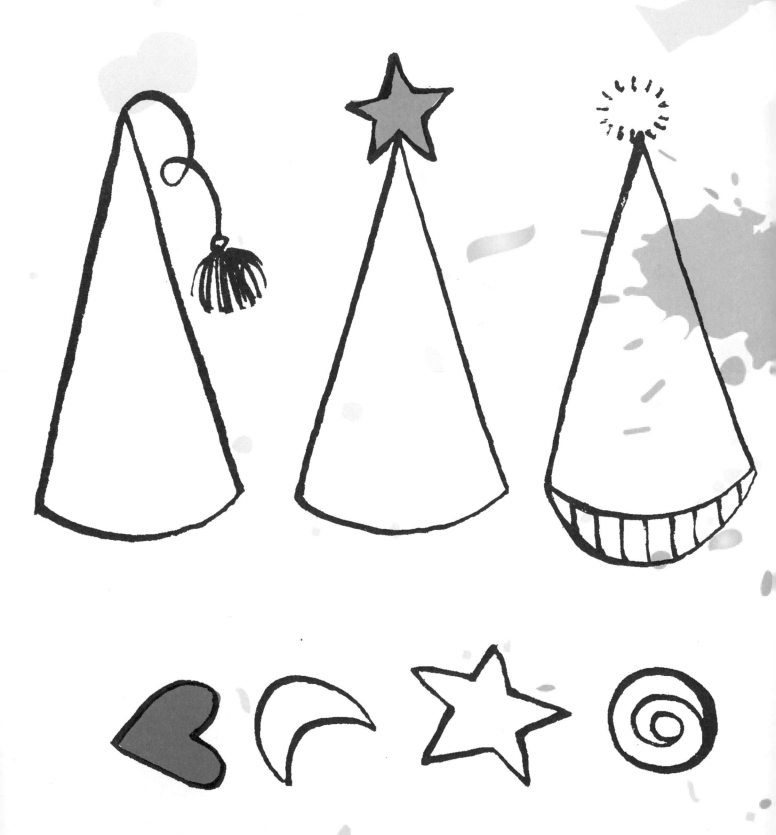

Now design your own.

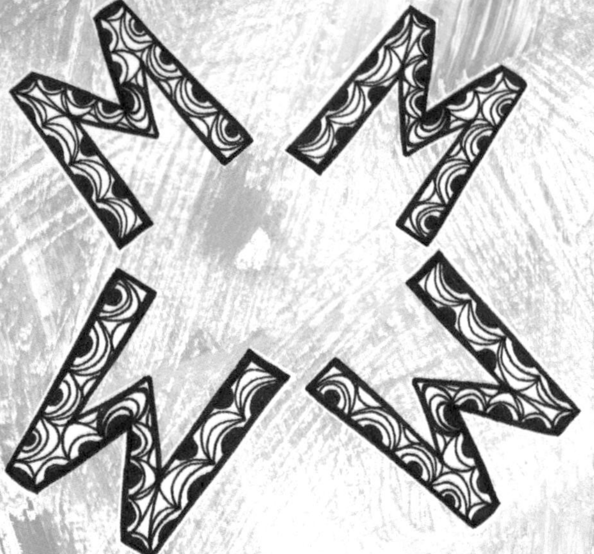

reversed

inverted

upside down

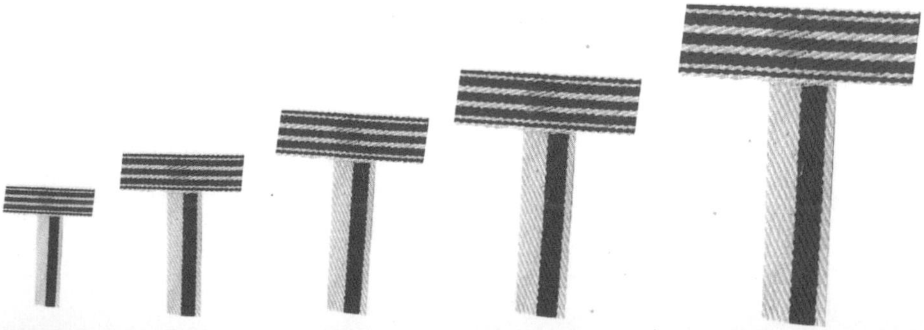

Using only letters, create a pattern.

inside out
back to front

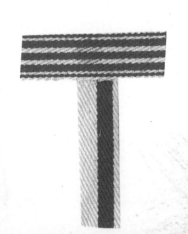
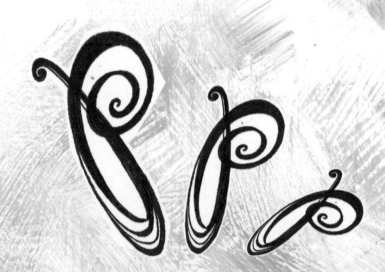

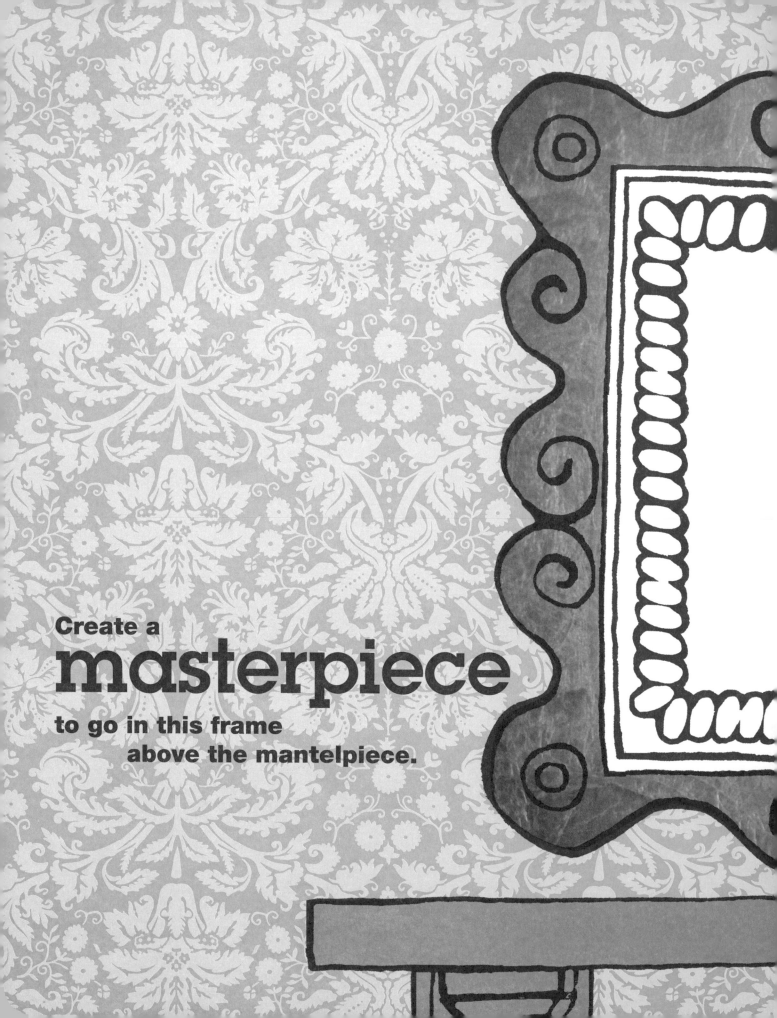

Create a
masterpiece
**to go in this frame
above the mantelpiece.**

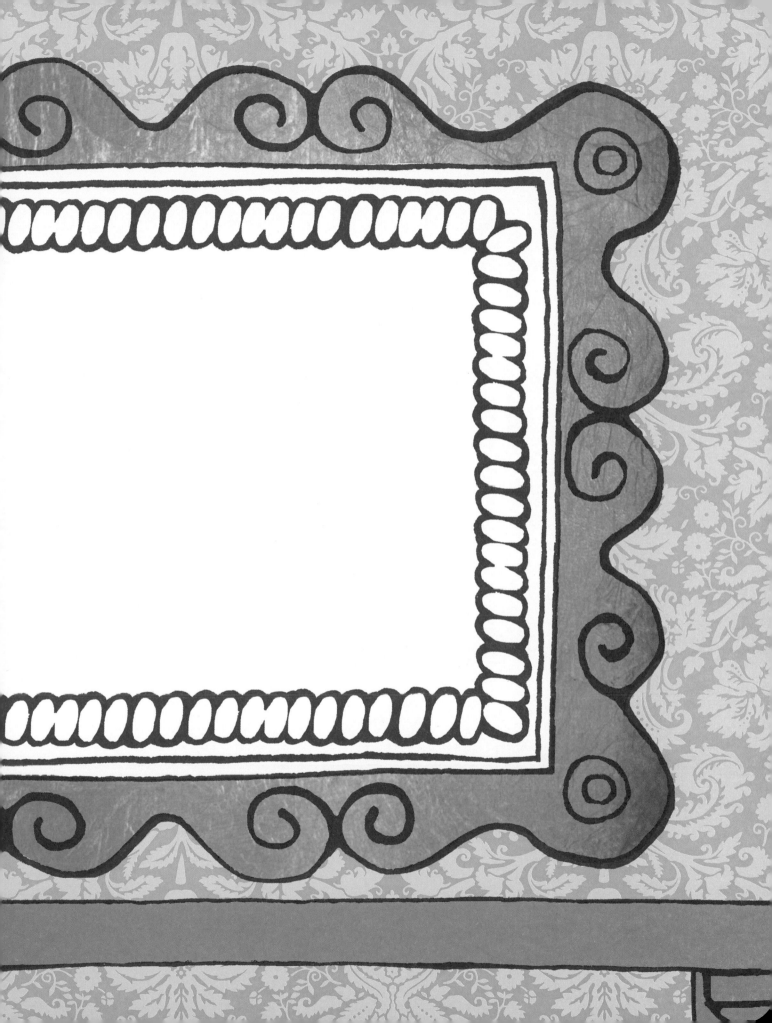

Create a *list of words* about water.

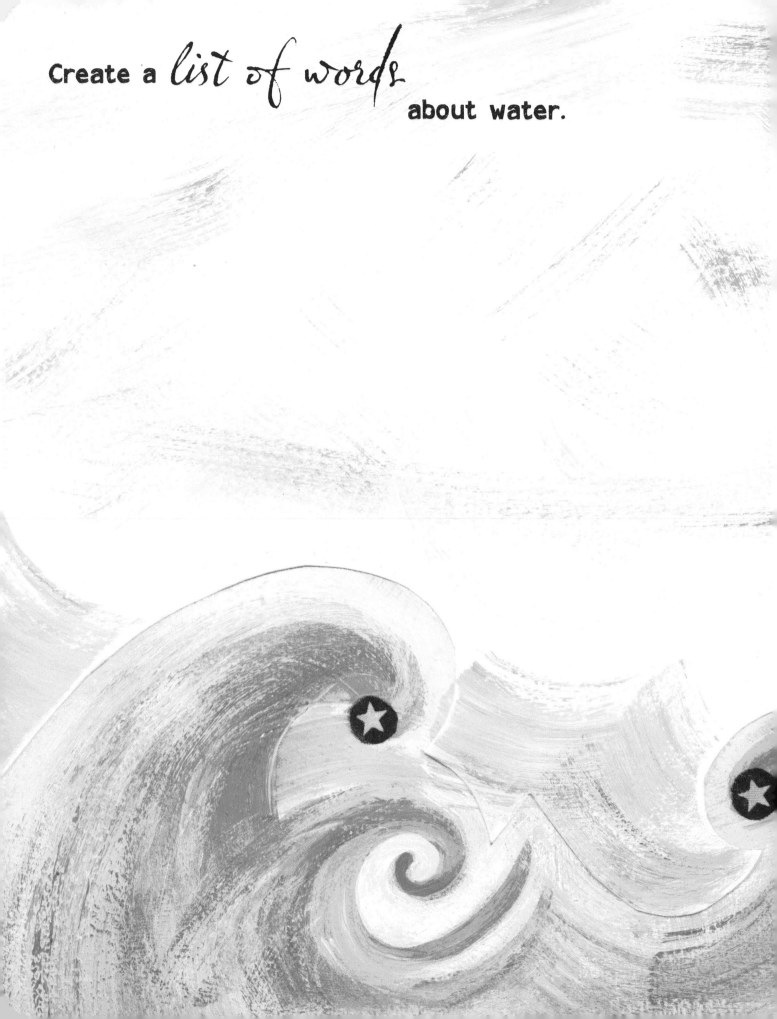

SUBMERGE those words into an ocean image.

Turn these shapes into fish.

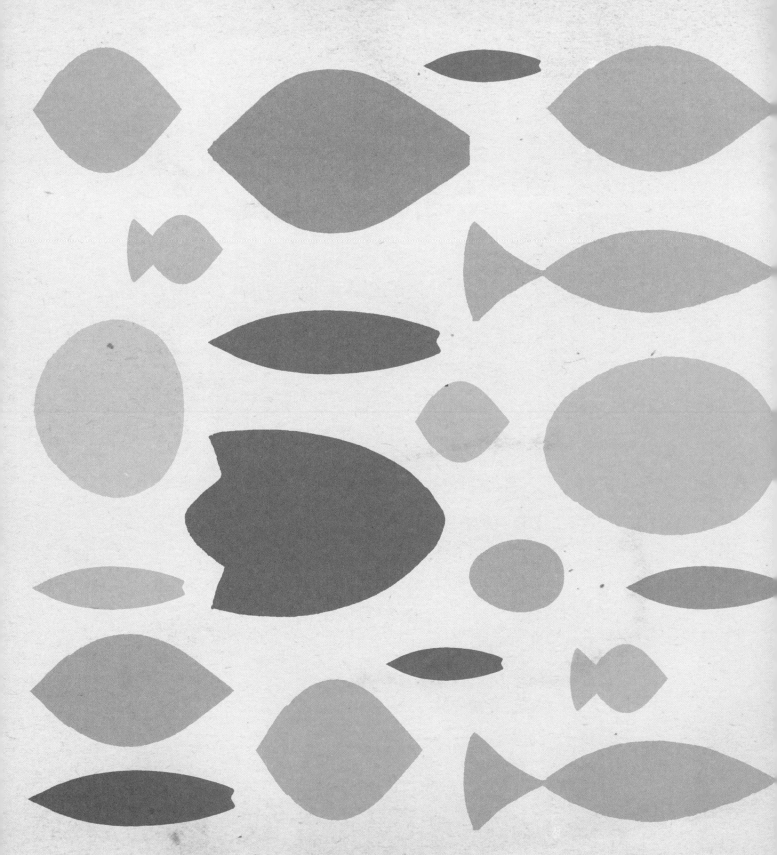

Draw a **brawl** between four colors.

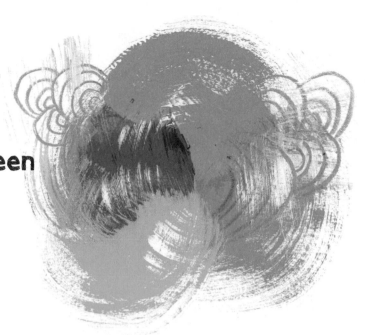

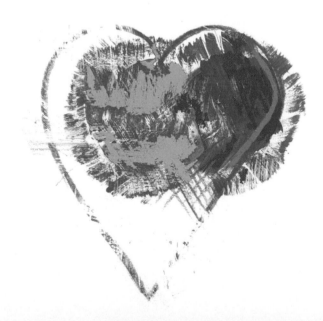

Color every other square.

Draw the **inside** of your house
from the **outside.**

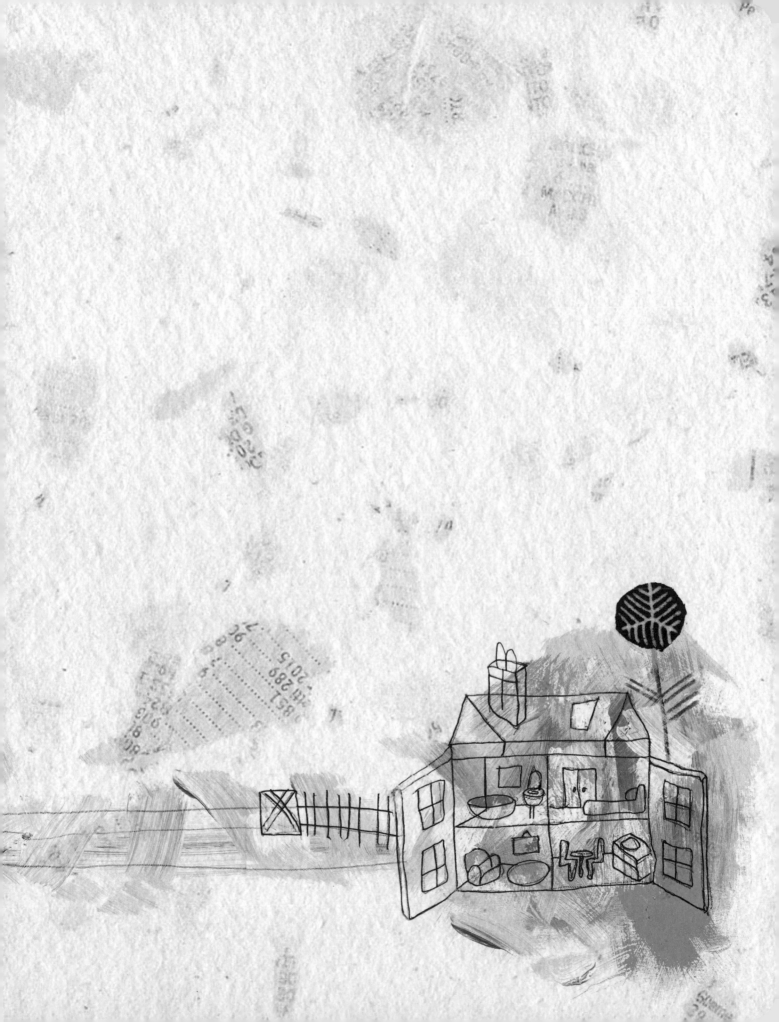

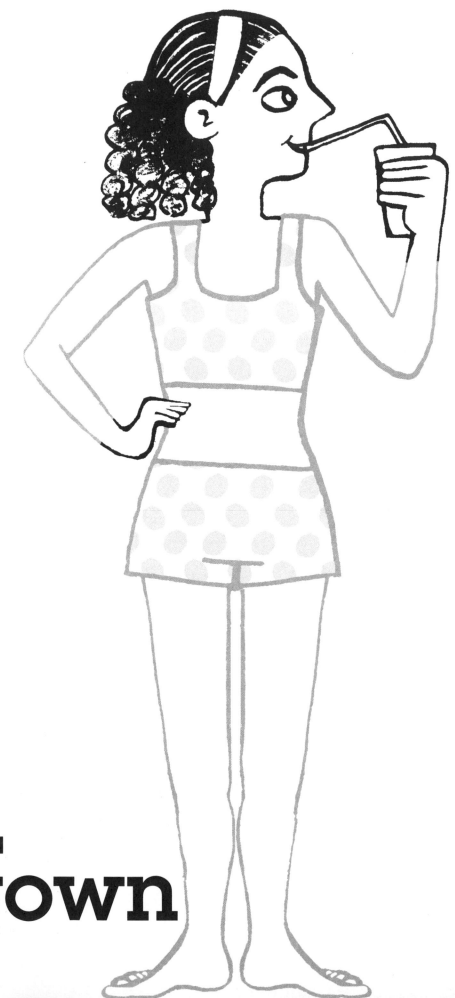

Design a beautiful
ball gown
for this girl.

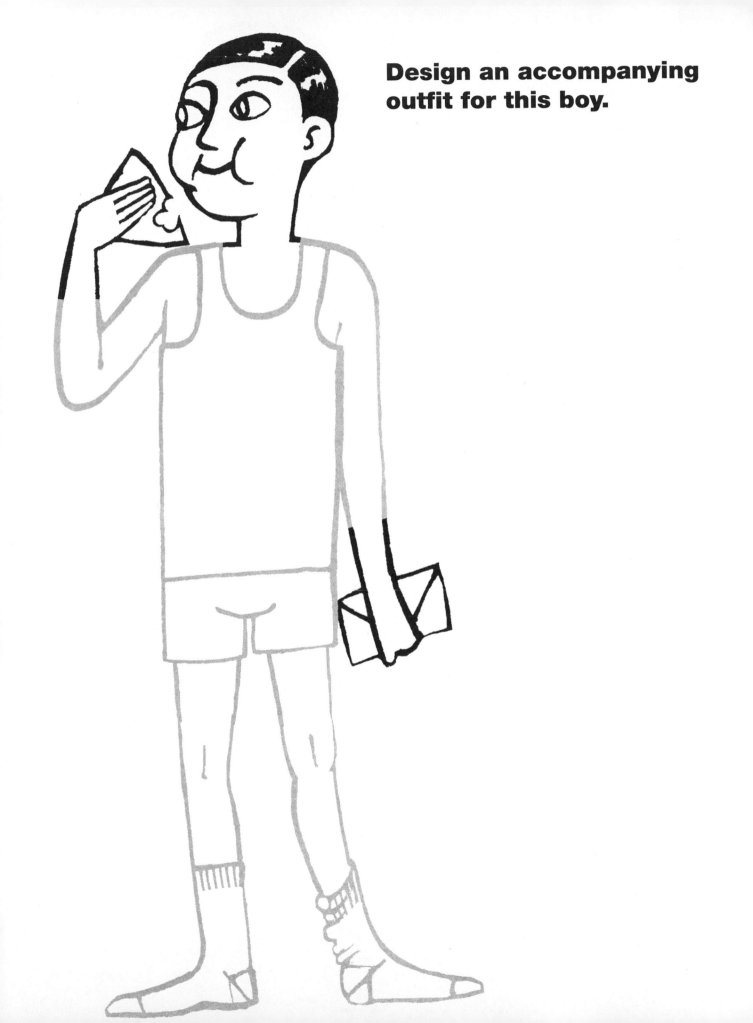

Design an accompanying outfit for this boy.

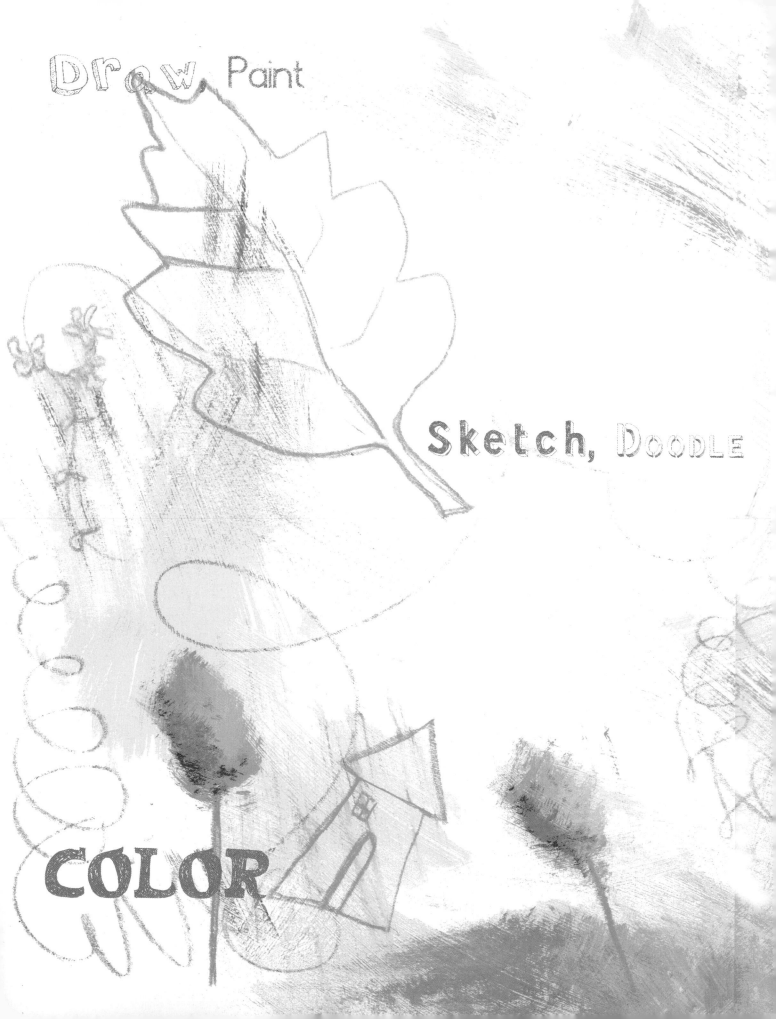

Draw, Paint

Sketch, Doodle

COLOR

Shade

Outline, Depict

Illustrate

Scribble, Jot

Doodle cats and dogs.

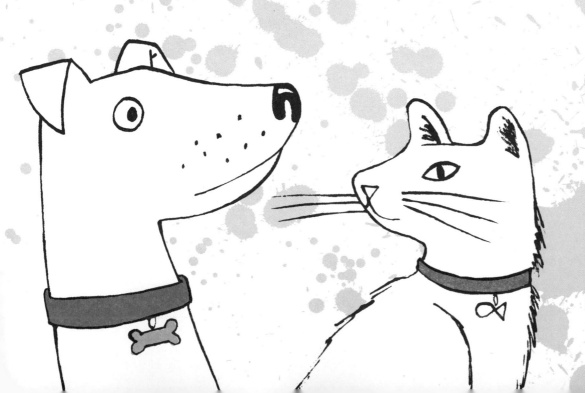

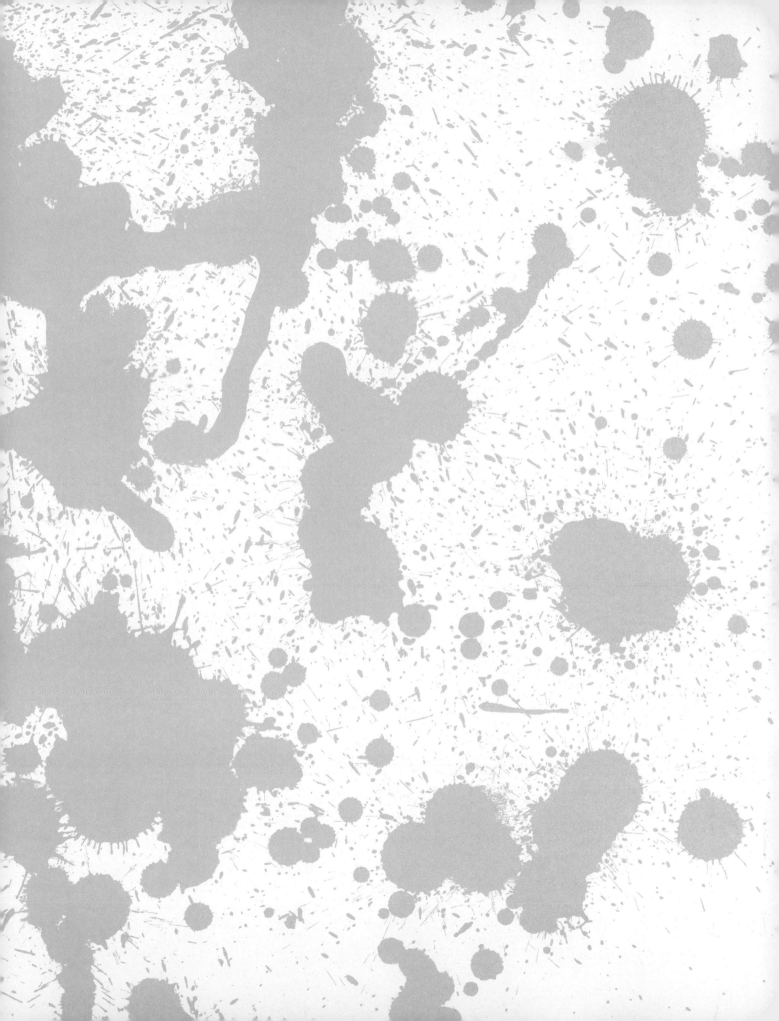

CREATE ANYTHING!

Draw clothes
drying on this clothesline.

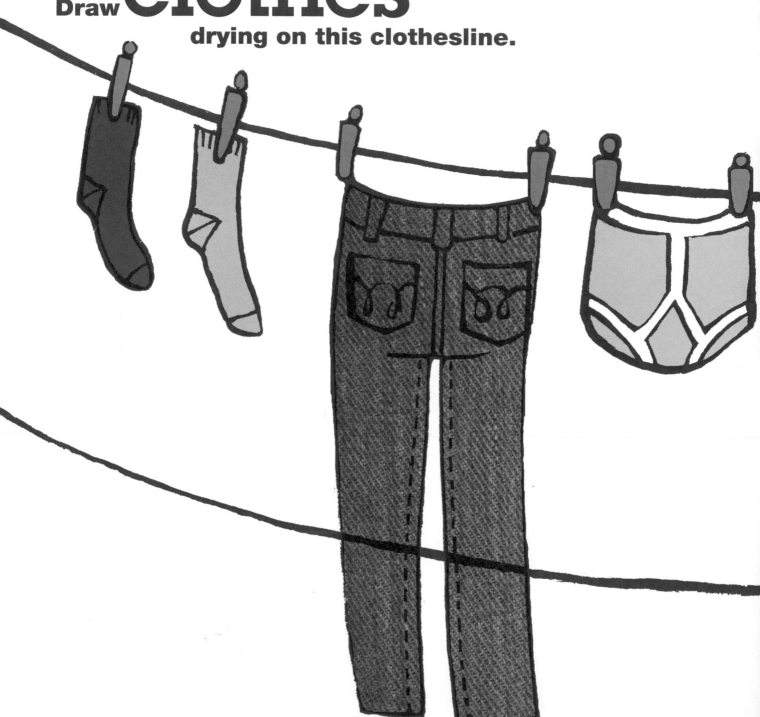

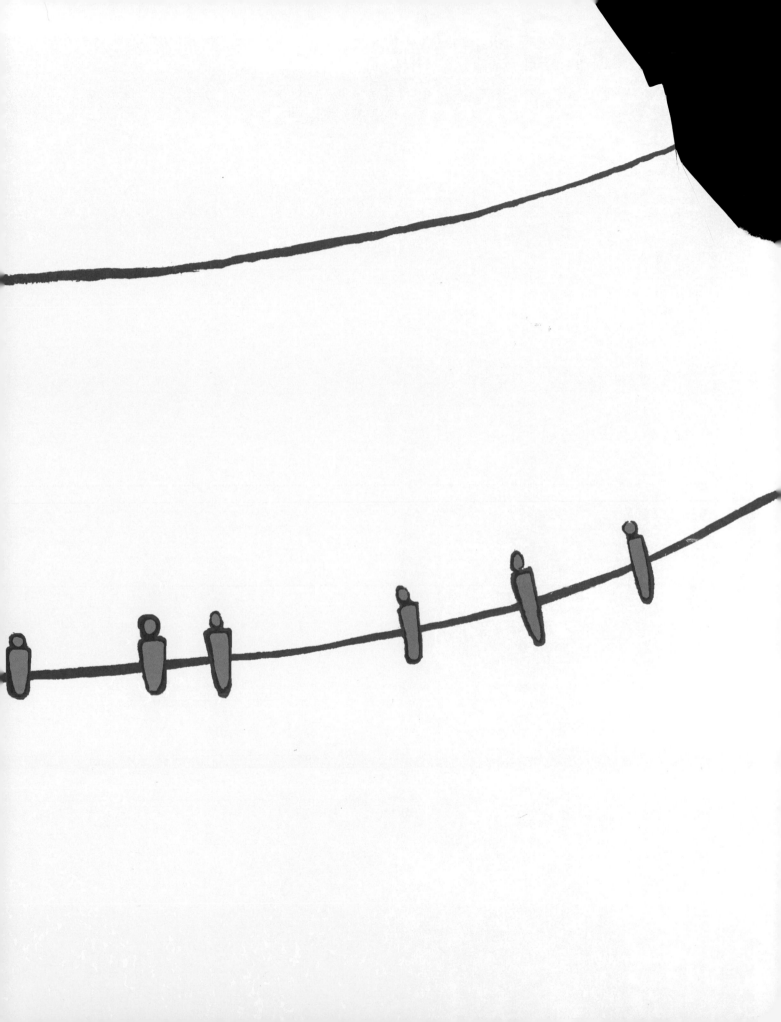

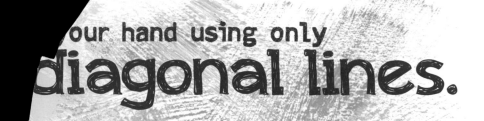

our hand using only

diagonal lines.

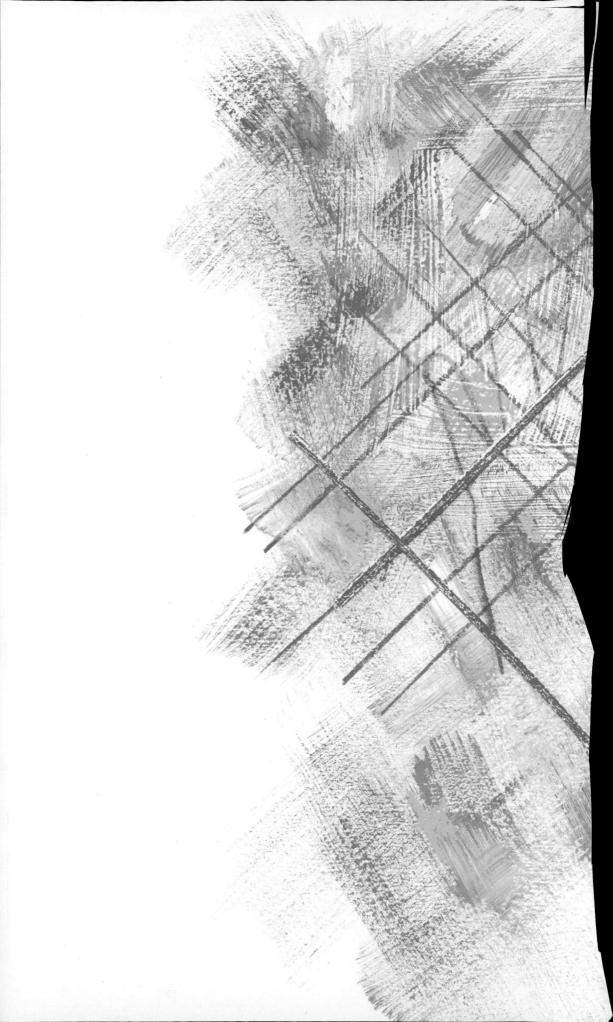

t's above and below the
sea level.

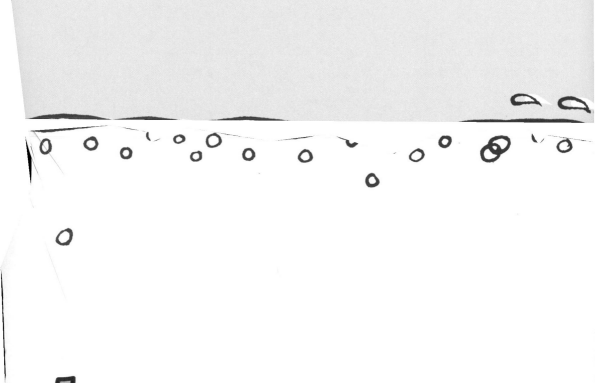

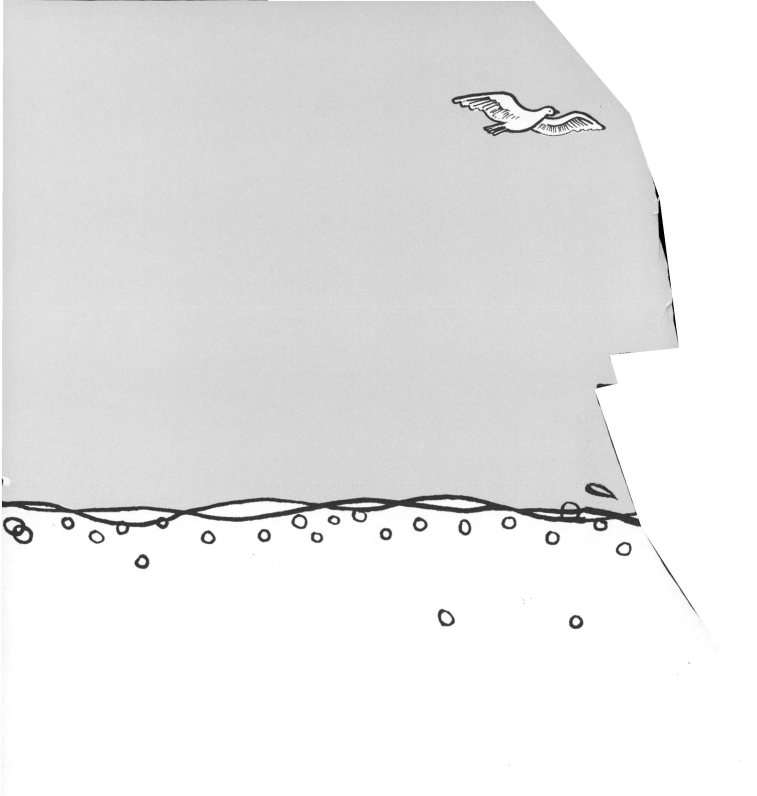

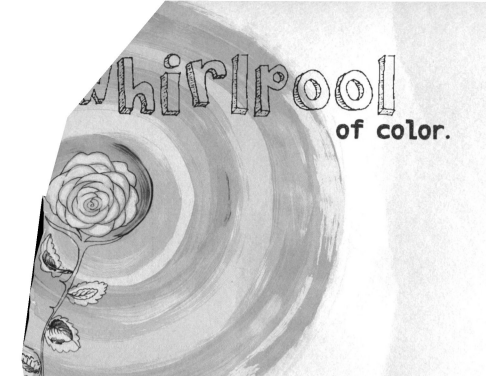

whirlpool

of color.

abstract art.

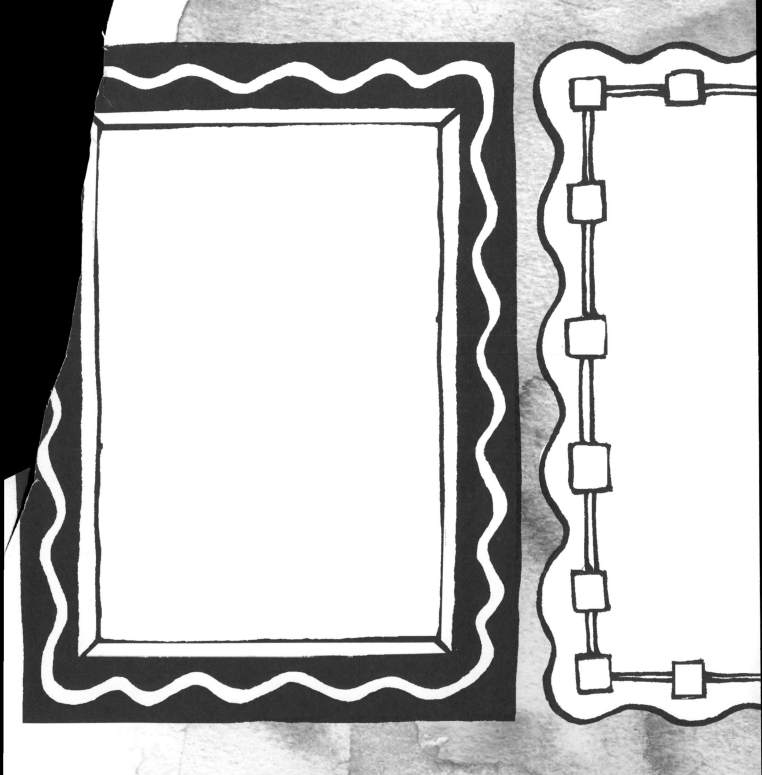

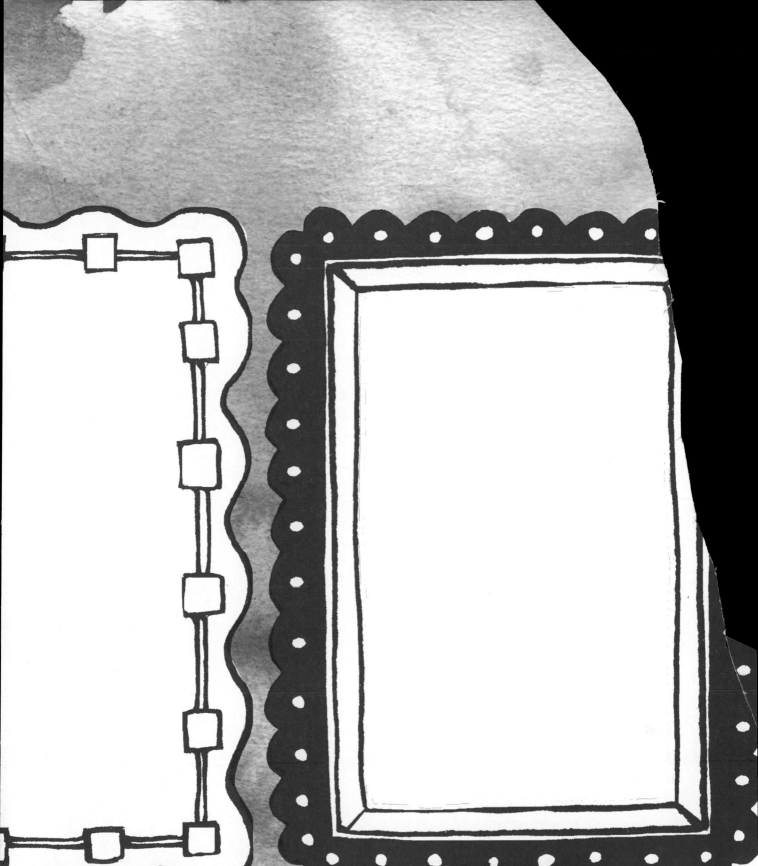

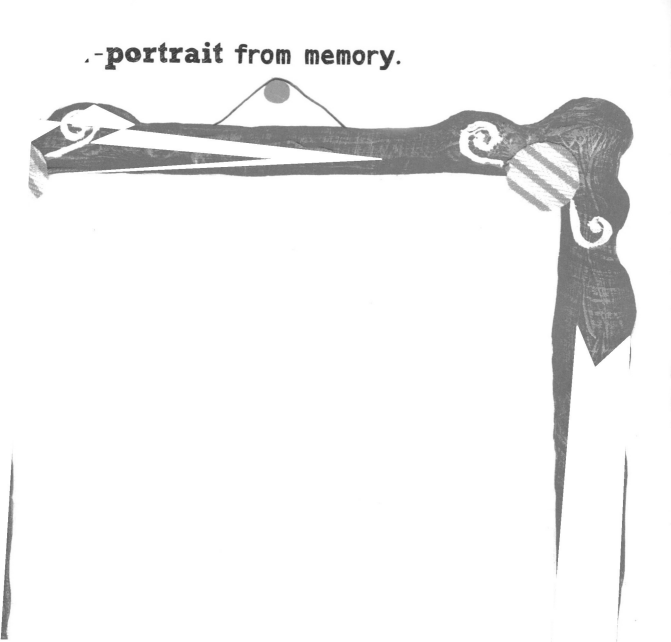

.-**portrait** from memory.

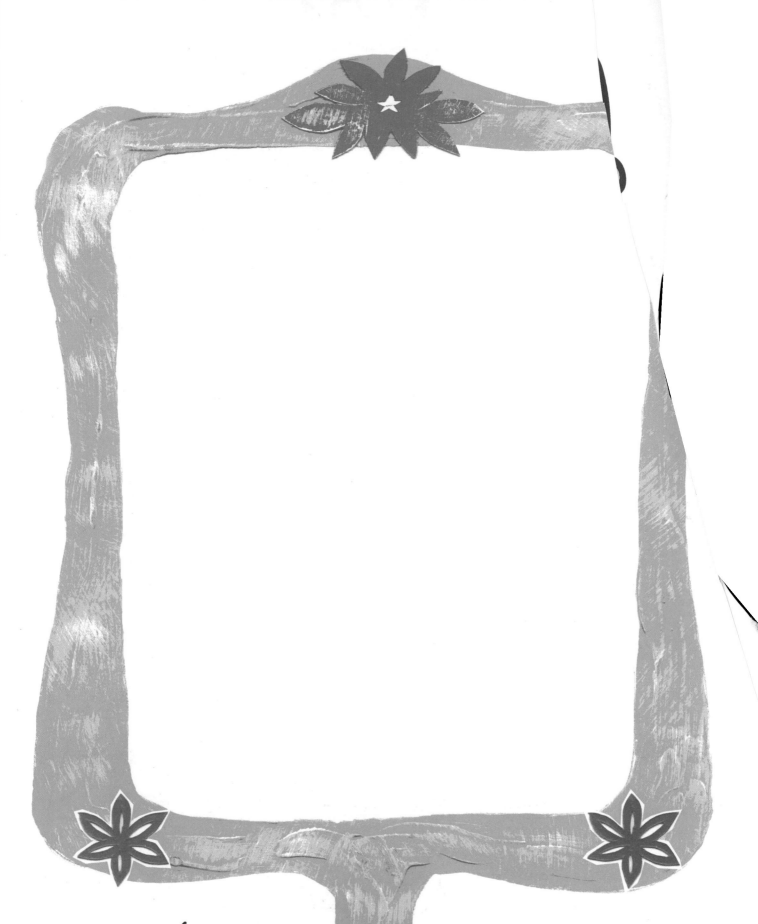

Draw a *self-portrait* using a mirror.

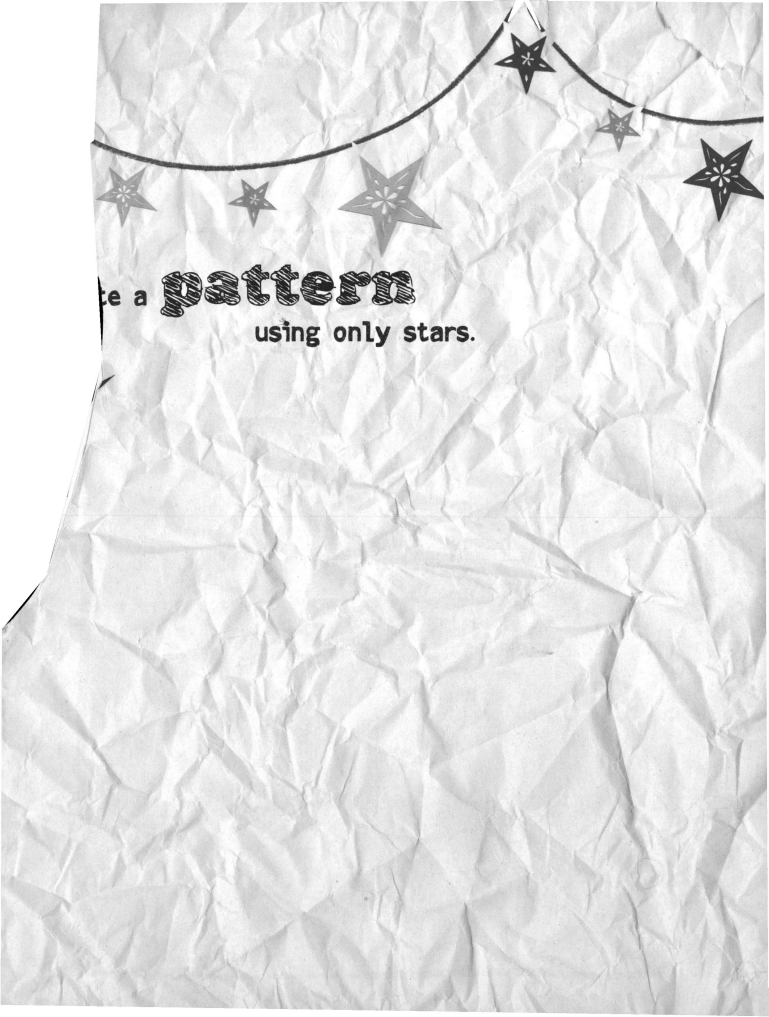

te a **pattern**

using only stars.

Draw this princess
a tower.

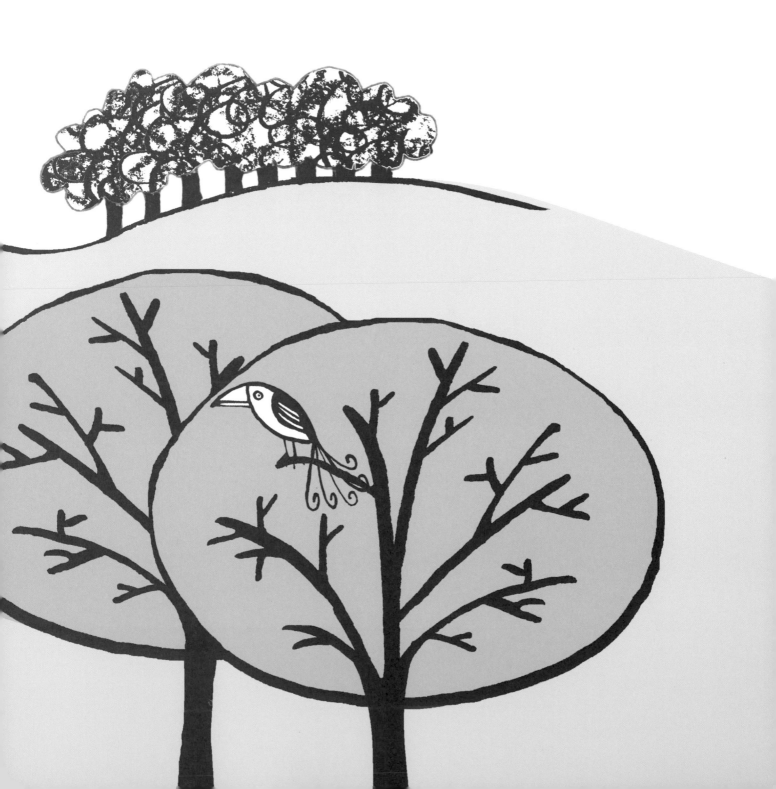

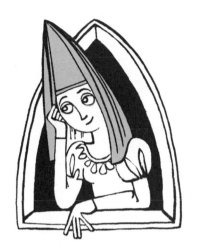
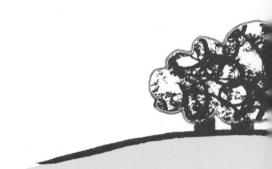

Doodle without taking your pen off the paper.

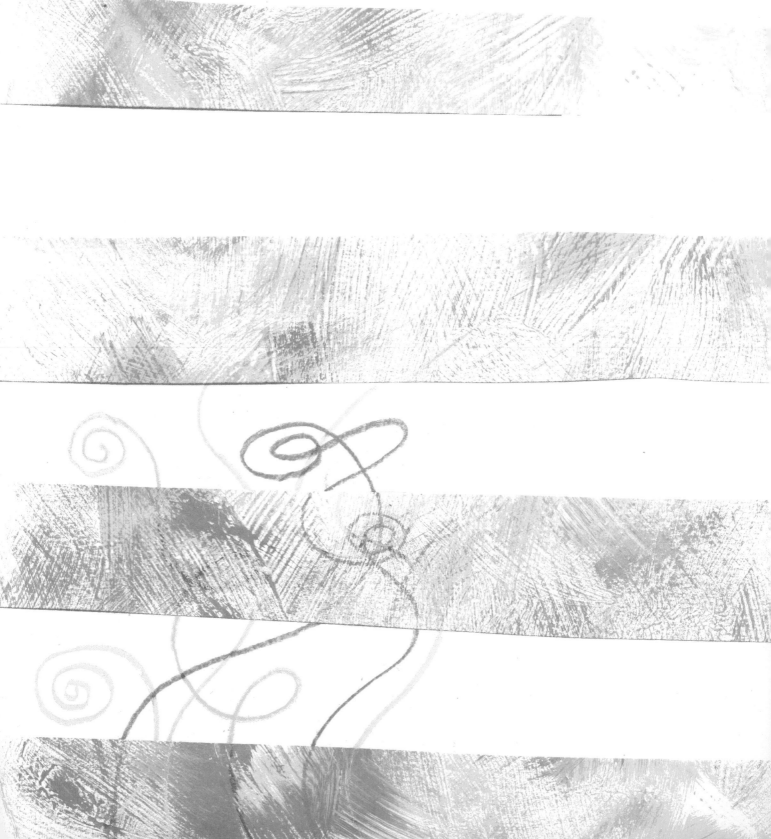

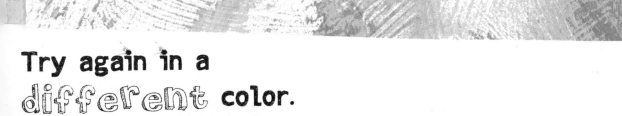

Try again in a
different color.

And again?

Fill these pages with
snowflakes.

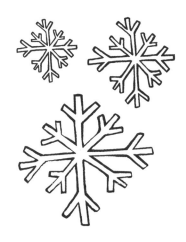

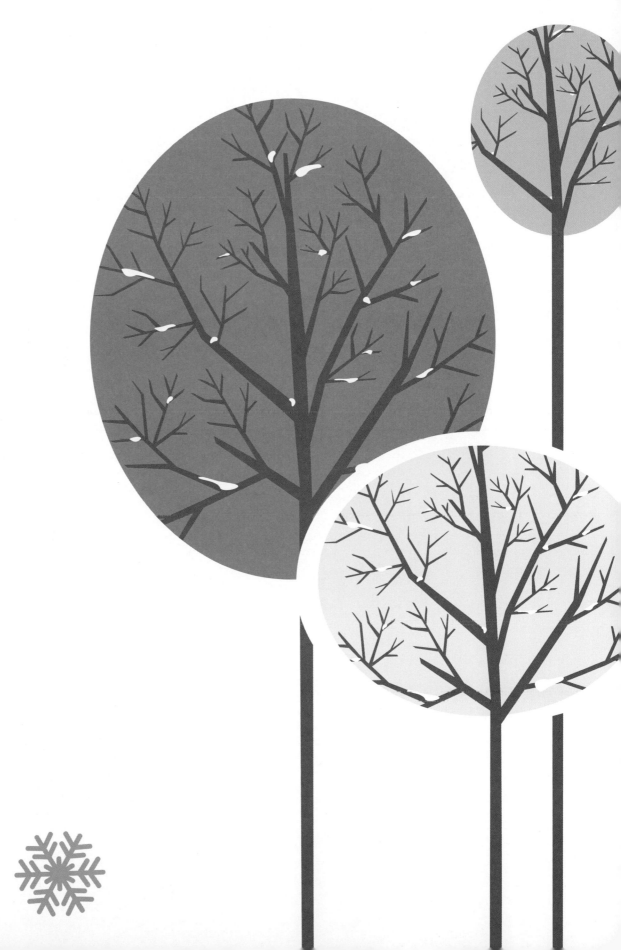

"Even if you can't draw, do a little doodle or rip an illustration from a magazine. These visuals will help bring your idea to life."

John Emmerling.

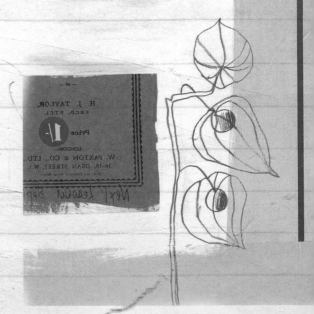

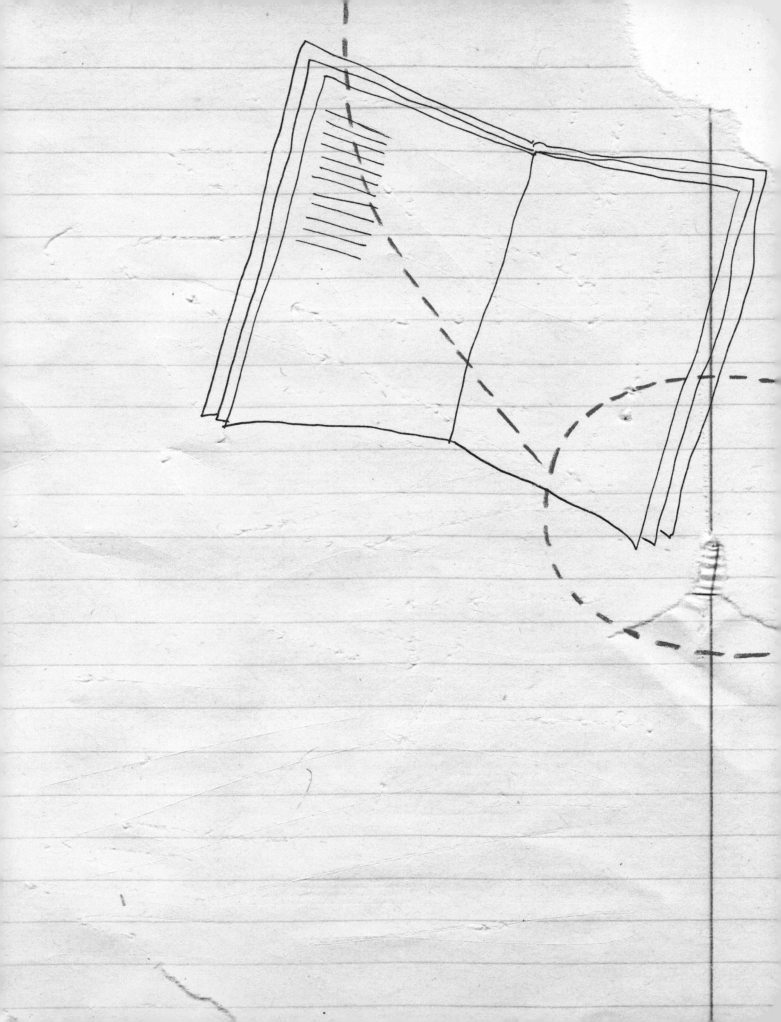

Draw fireworks.

Fill these pages with
fairies.

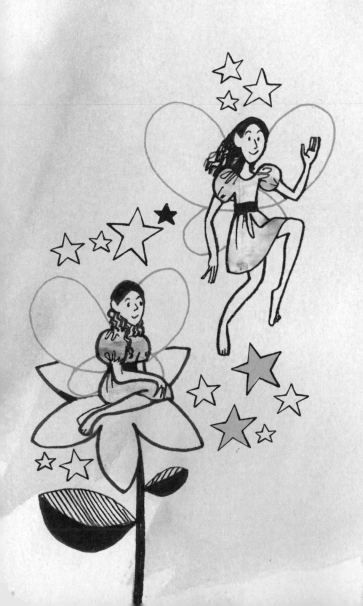

Graffiti these pages.

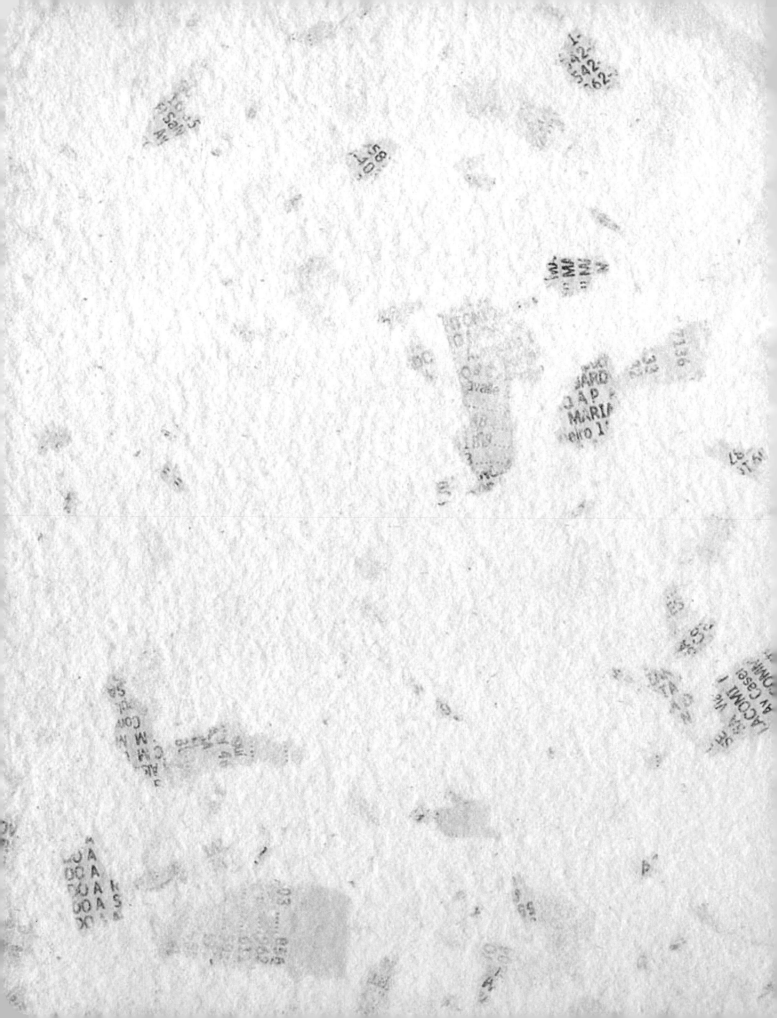

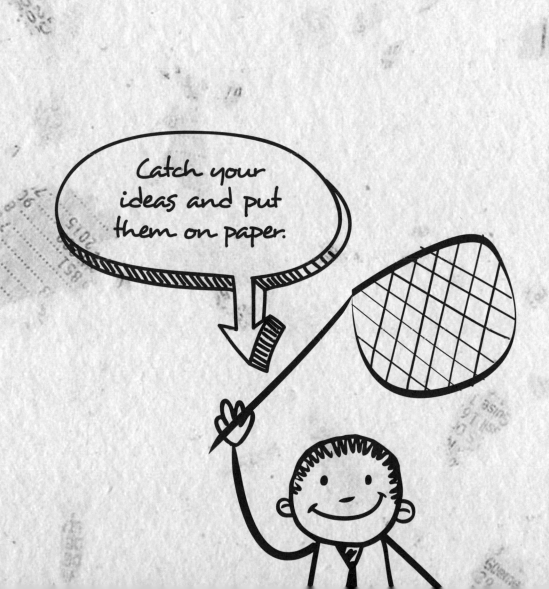

Draw your home using only wavy lines.

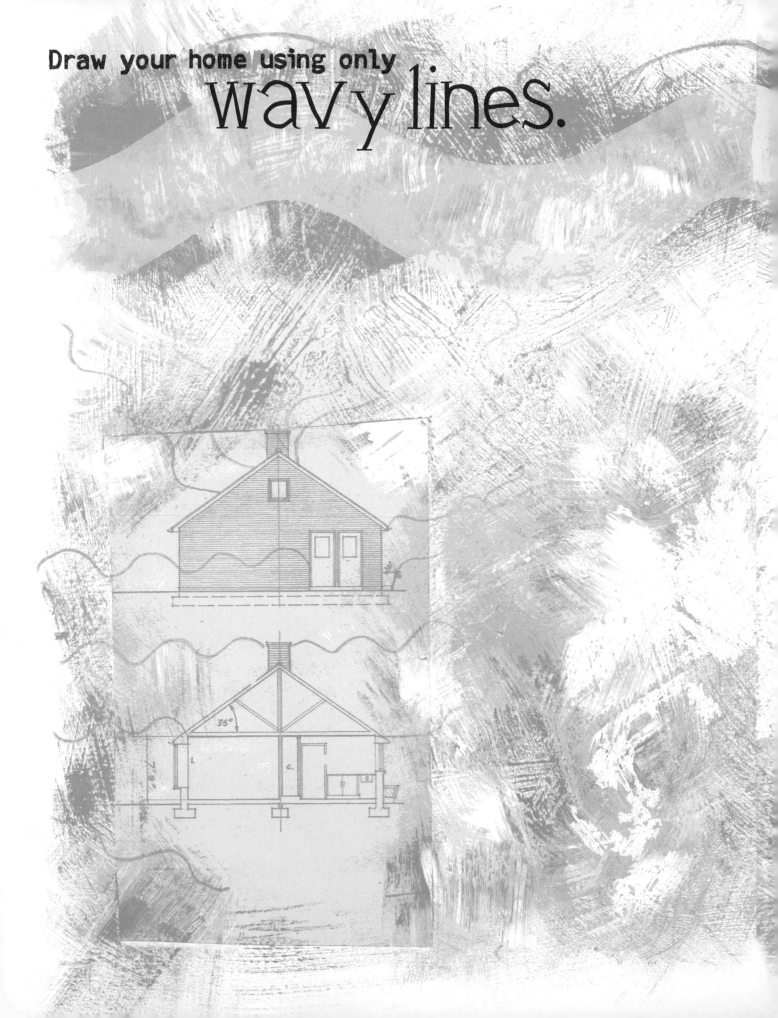

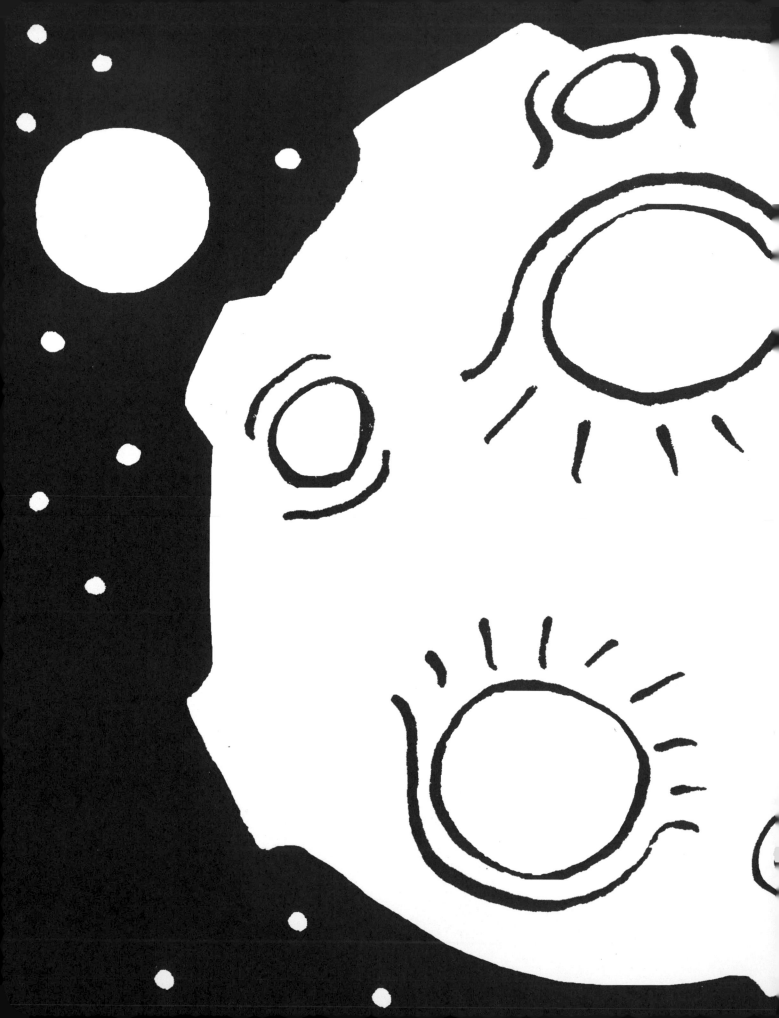

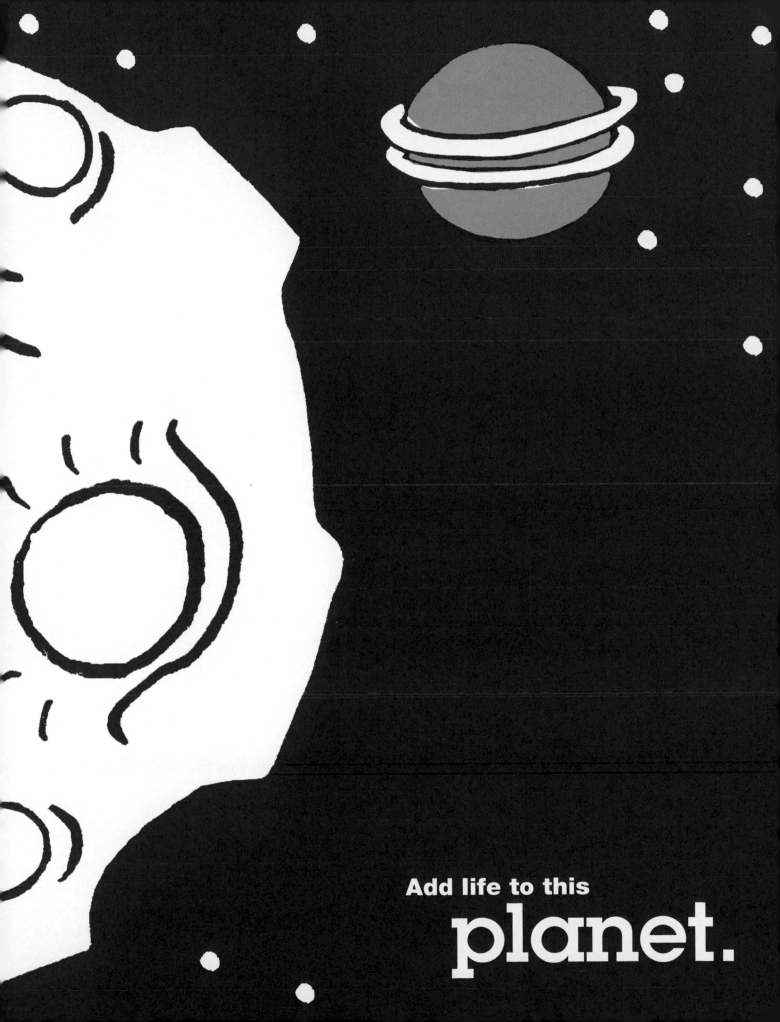

Add life to this
planet.

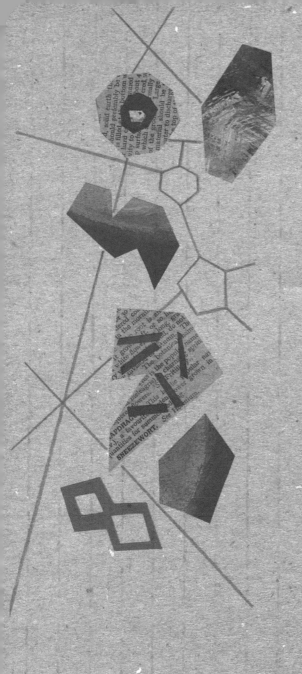

Fill these pages
with SHAPES that have
more than four sides.

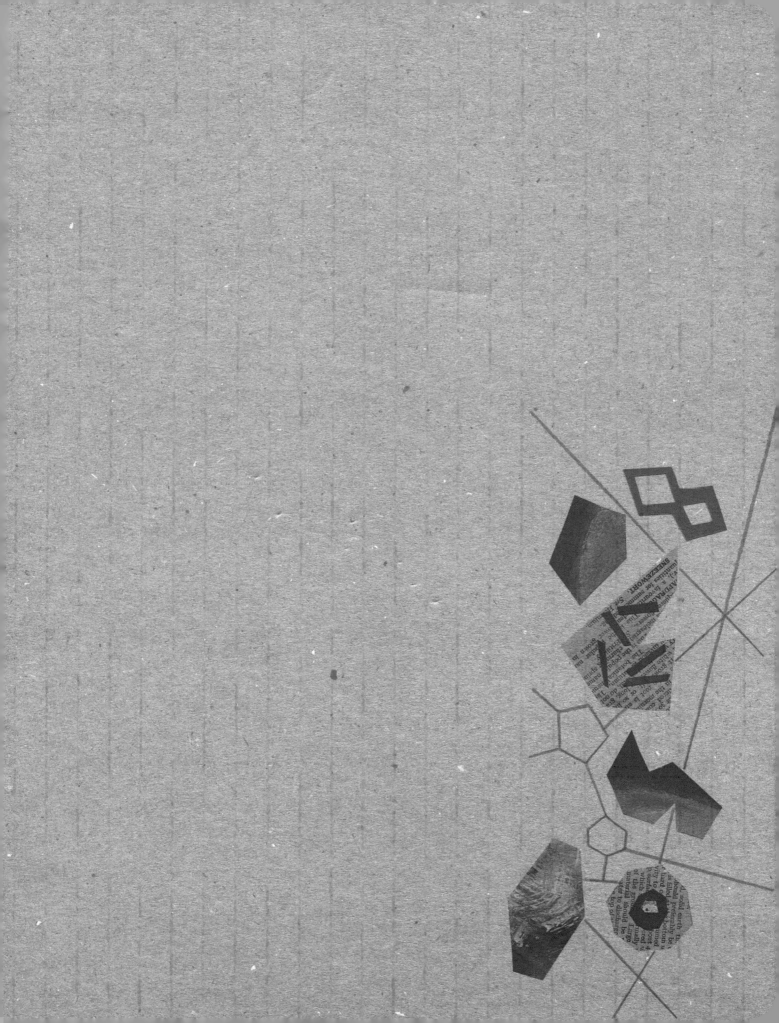

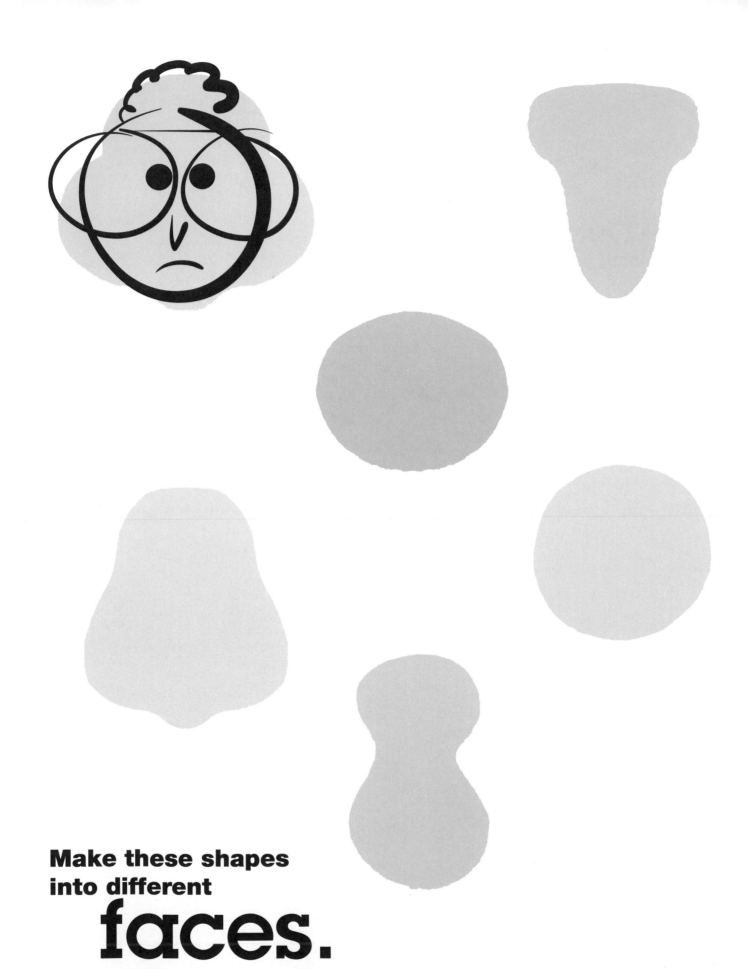

**Make these shapes
into different
faces.**

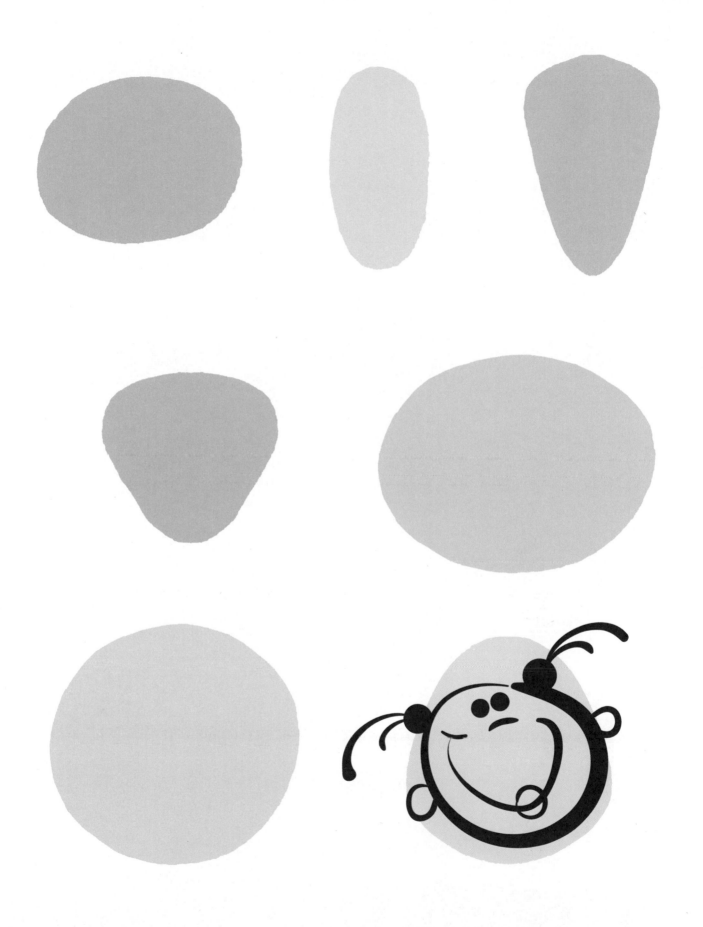

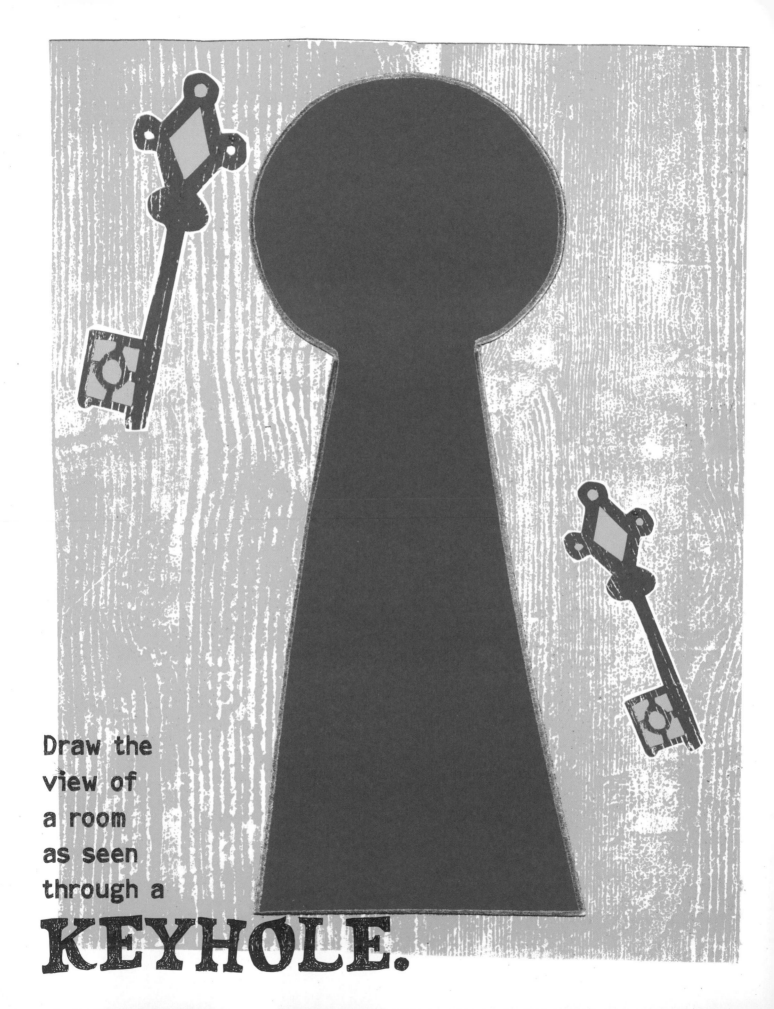

Draw the view of a room as seen through a

KEYHOLE.

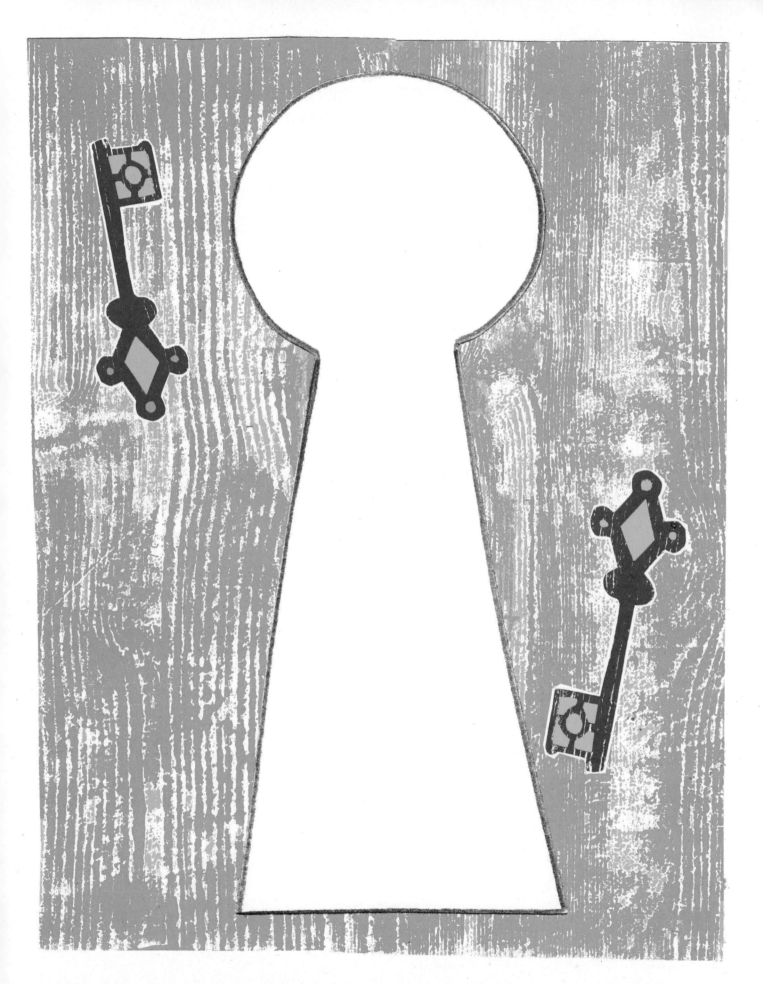

Draw the ingredients for your favorite meal.

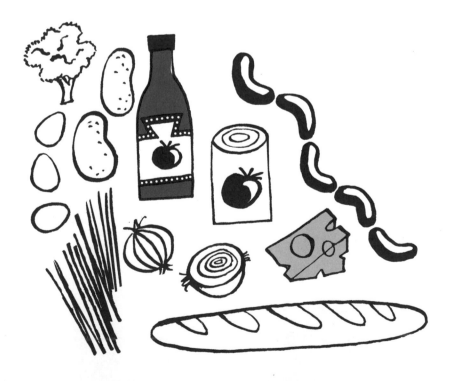

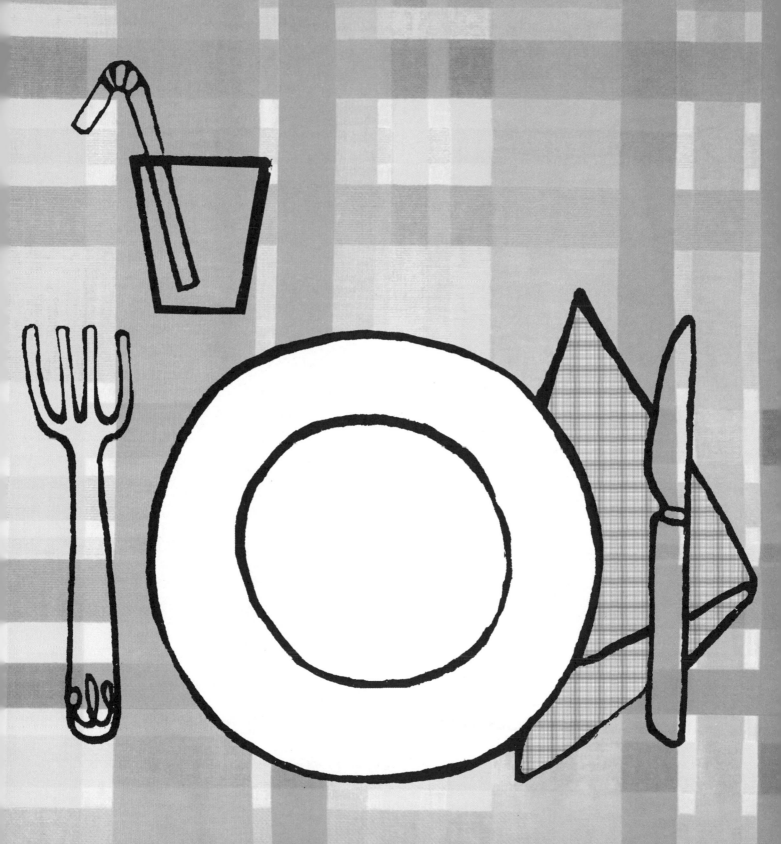

Fill this plate with your favorite food.

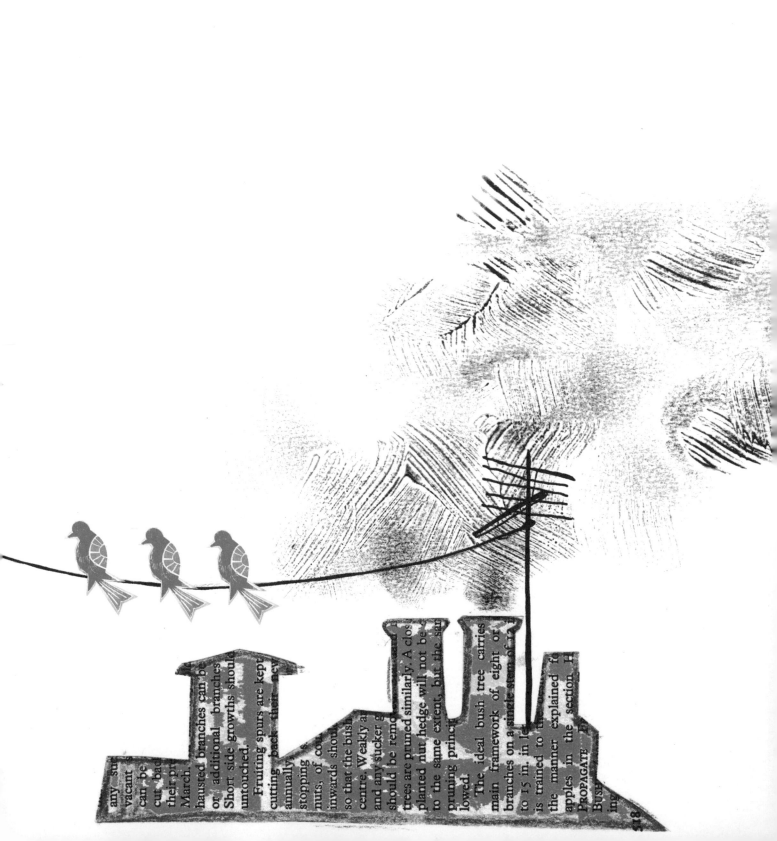

Fill these pages with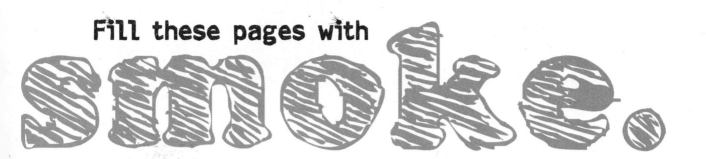

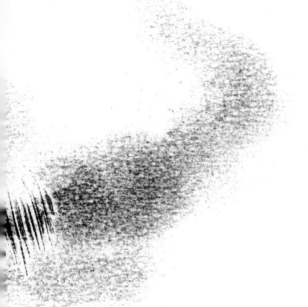

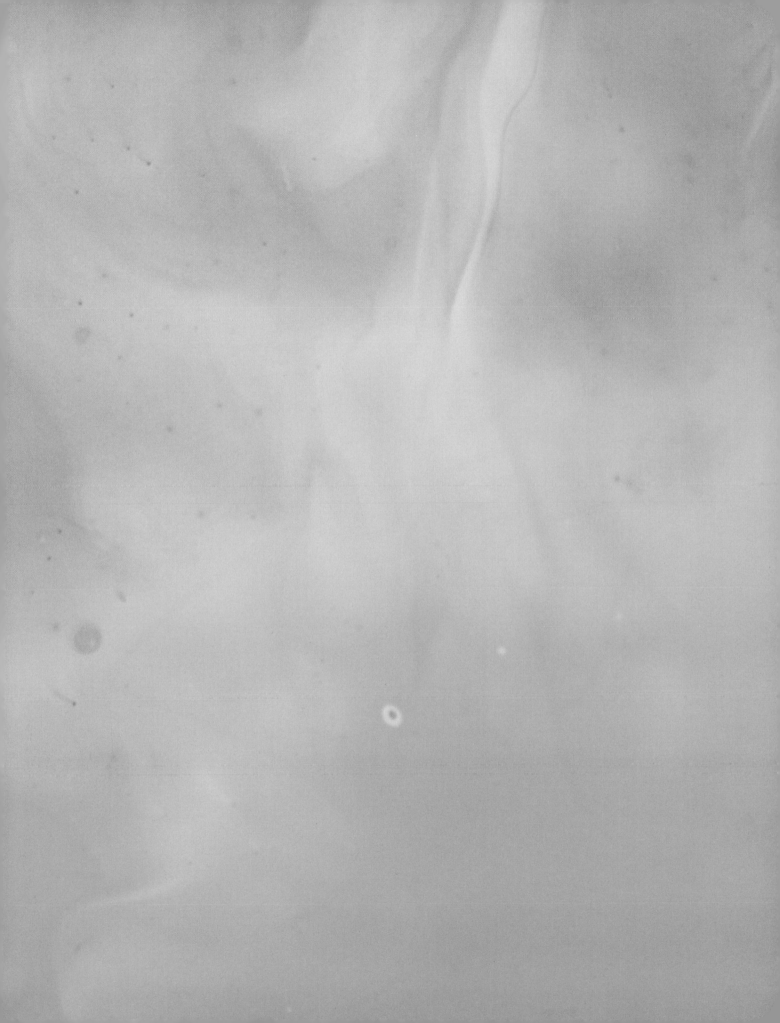

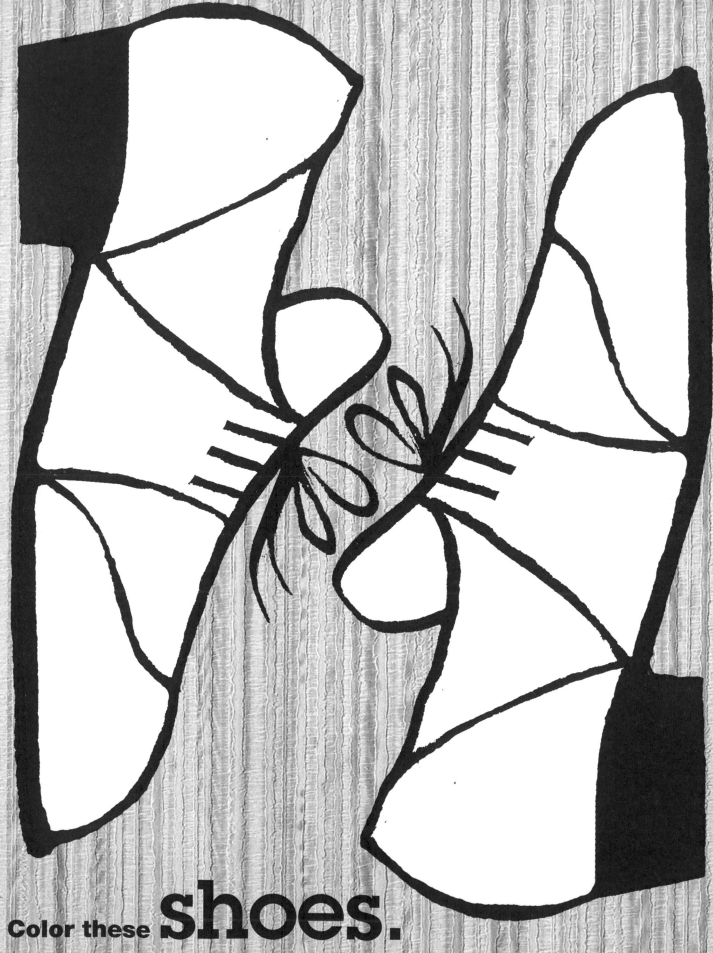

Color these shoes.

Now design your own.

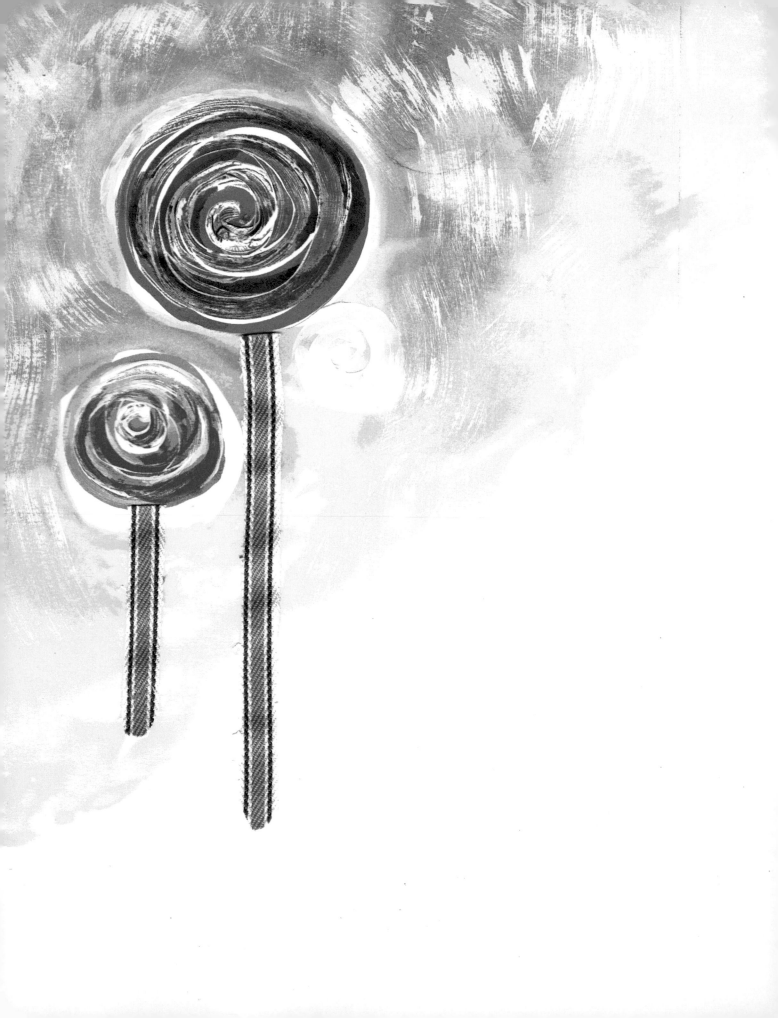

Fill these pages with
spirals.

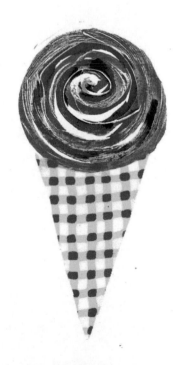

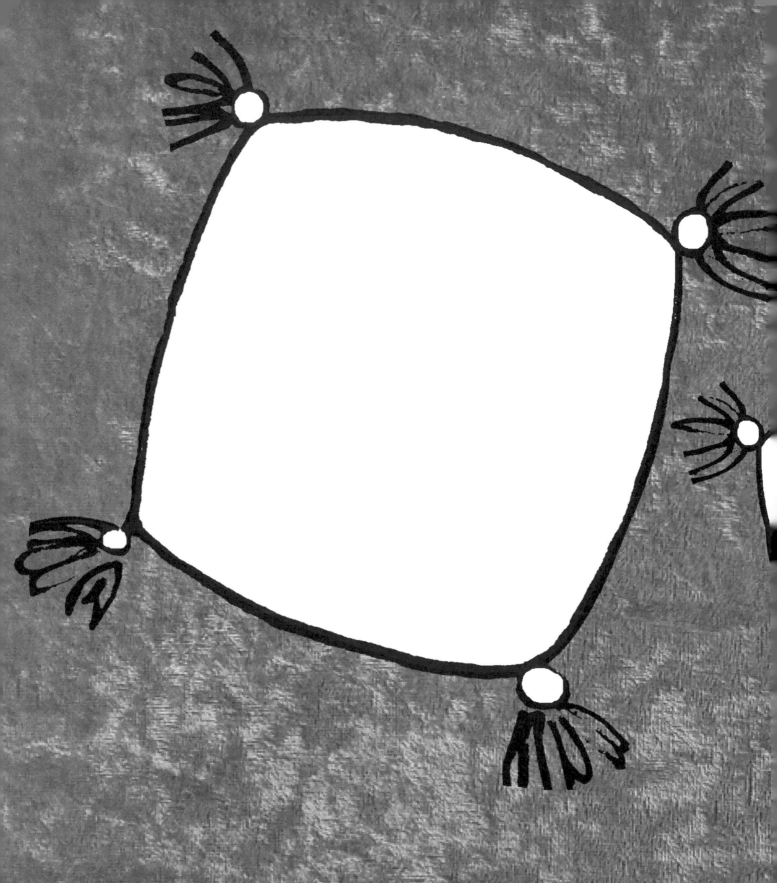

Design these pillows.

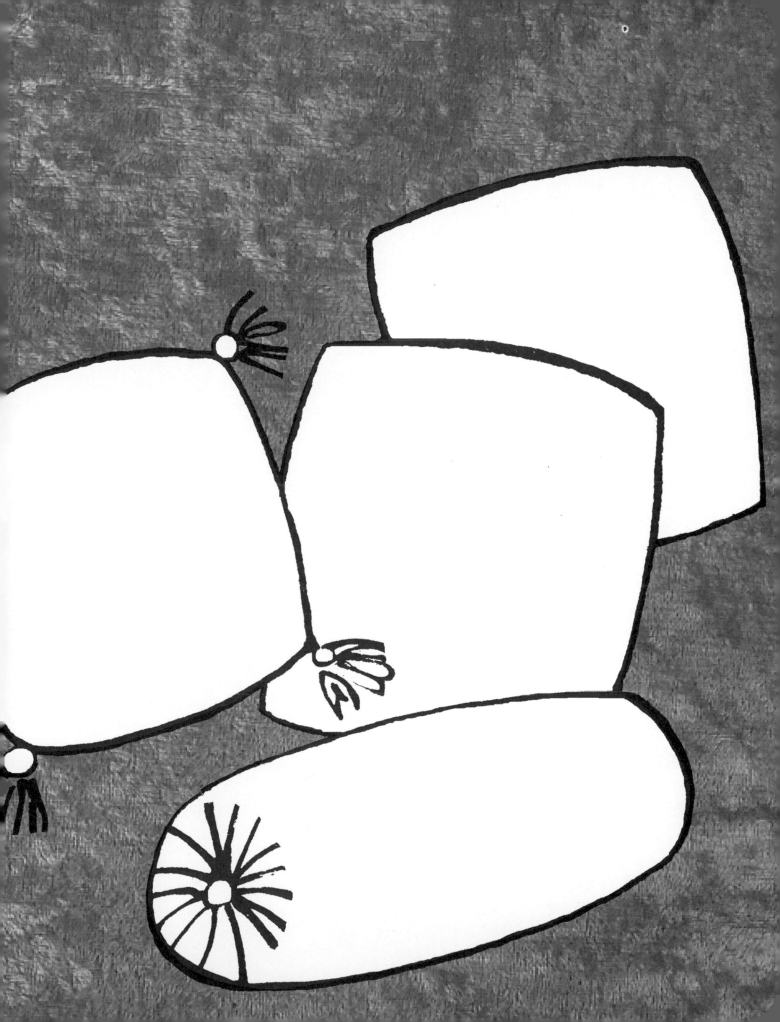

Draw your mood.

LOVE, SUBMISSION,
REMORSE, CONTEM
OPTIMISM, SERE
APPREHENSIO
PENSIVENESS, BOR
INTEREST, JO
SURPRISE, SADNES
ANTICIPATION, ECS
TERROR, AMAZEME
RAGE, V

WE, DISAPPROVAL,
, AGGRESSIVENESS,
TY, ACCEPTANCE,
DISTRACTION,
OM, ANNOYANCE,
TRUST, FEAR,
, DISGUST, ANGER,
ASY, ADMIRATION,
, GRIEF, LOATHING,
ILANCE.

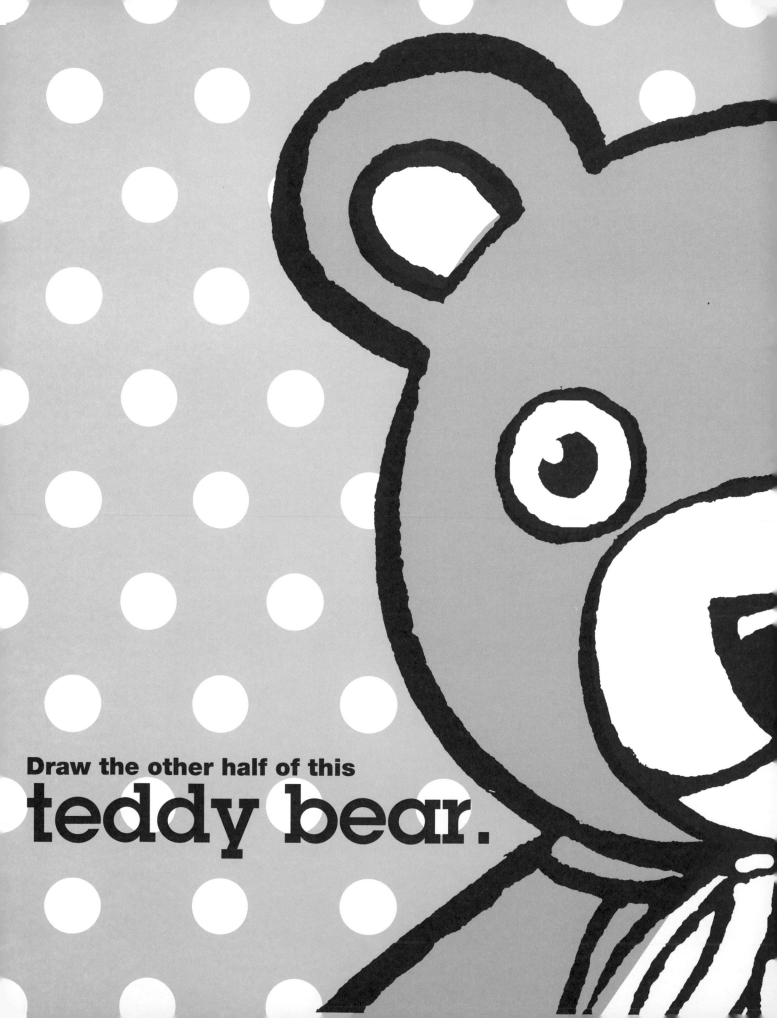

Draw the other half of this
teddy bear.

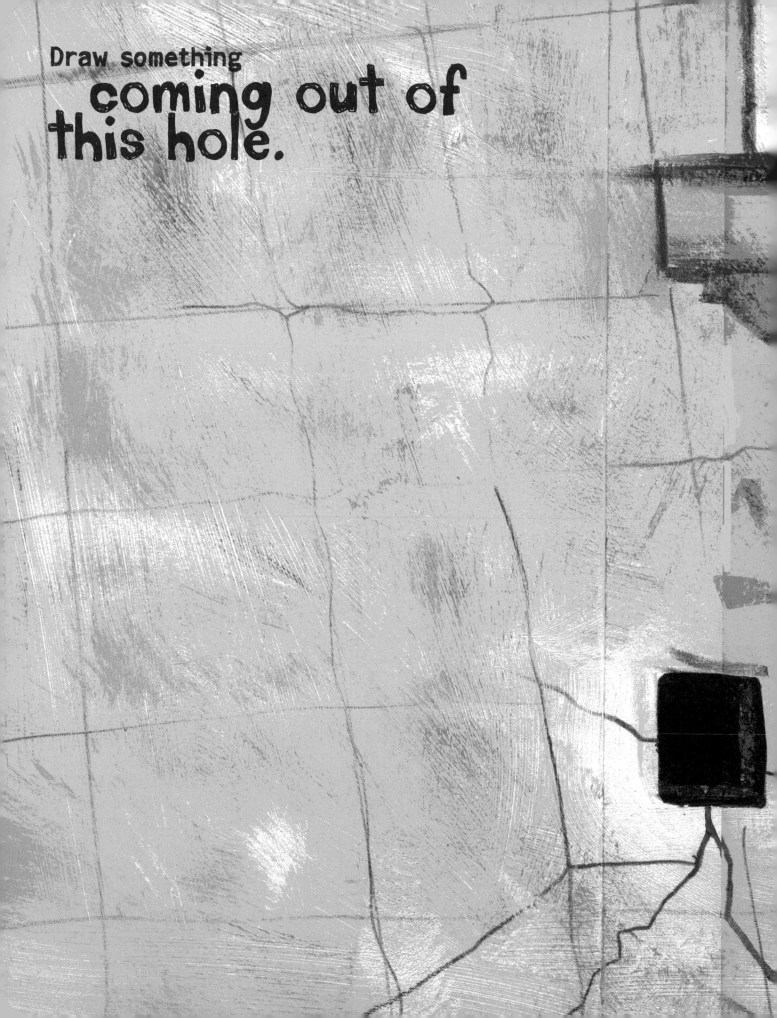

Draw something **coming out of this hole.**

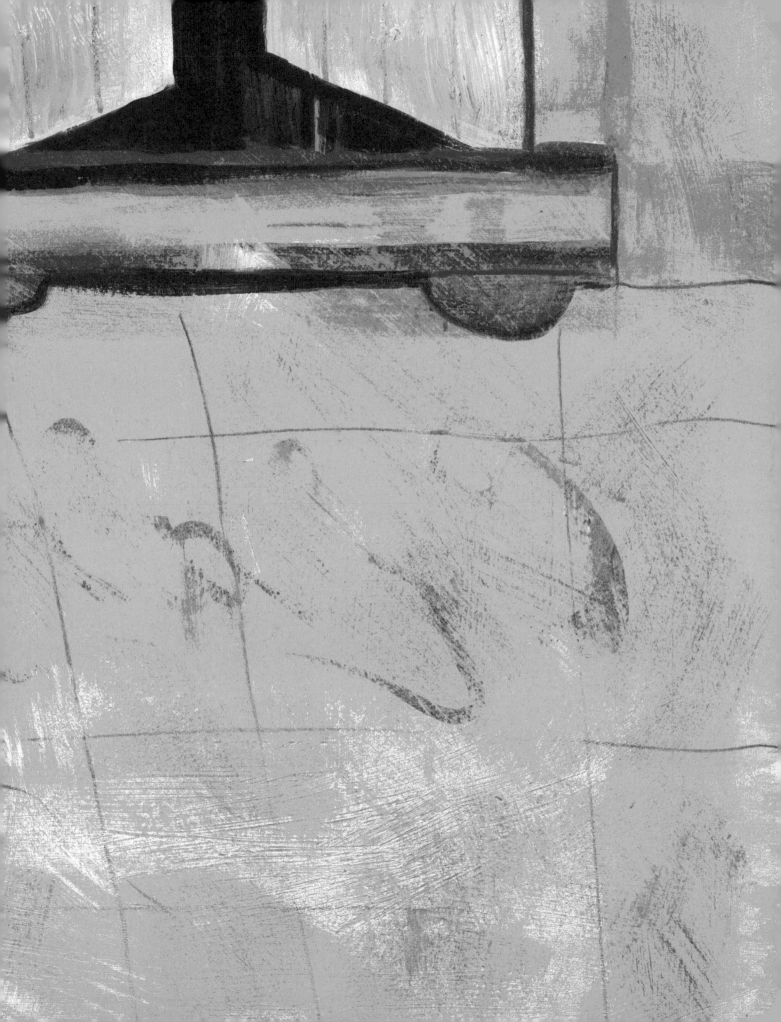

Add more vehicles to create a
traffic jam.

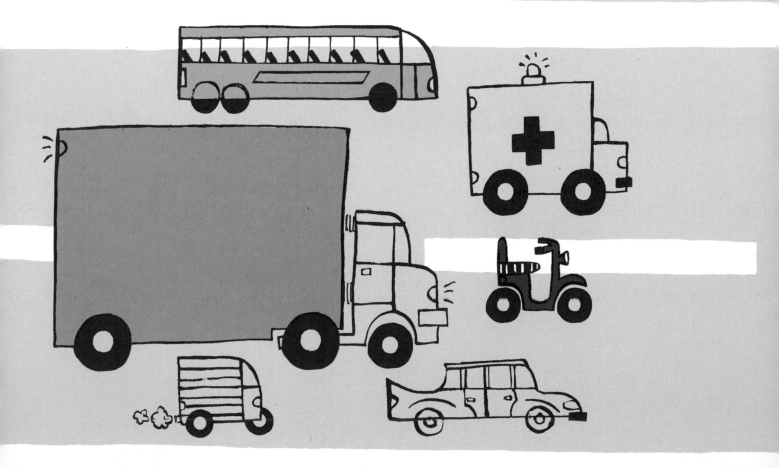

INSPIRE
YOURSELF.

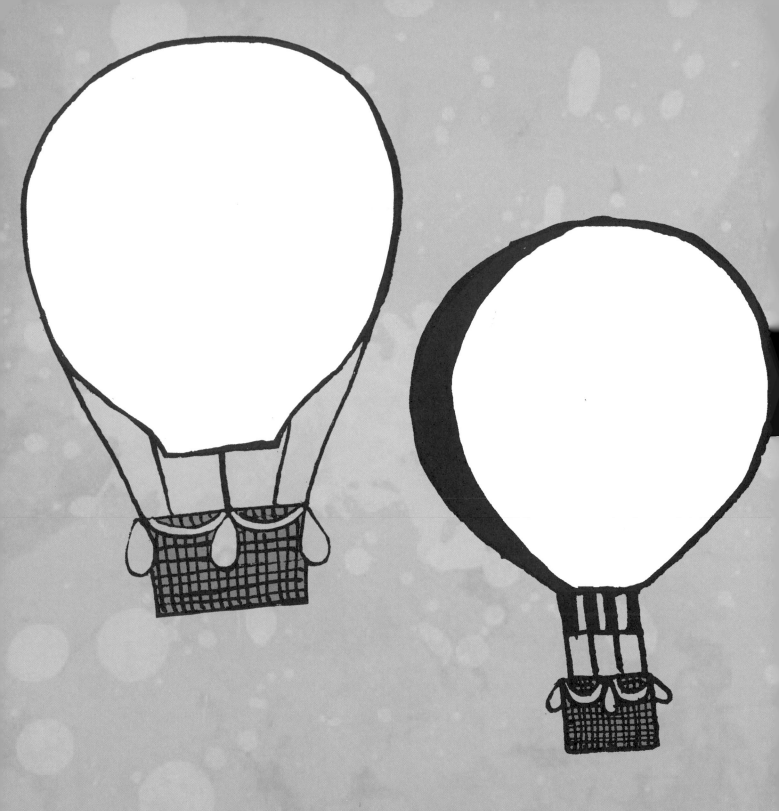

Design the **hot-air balloons** in this race.

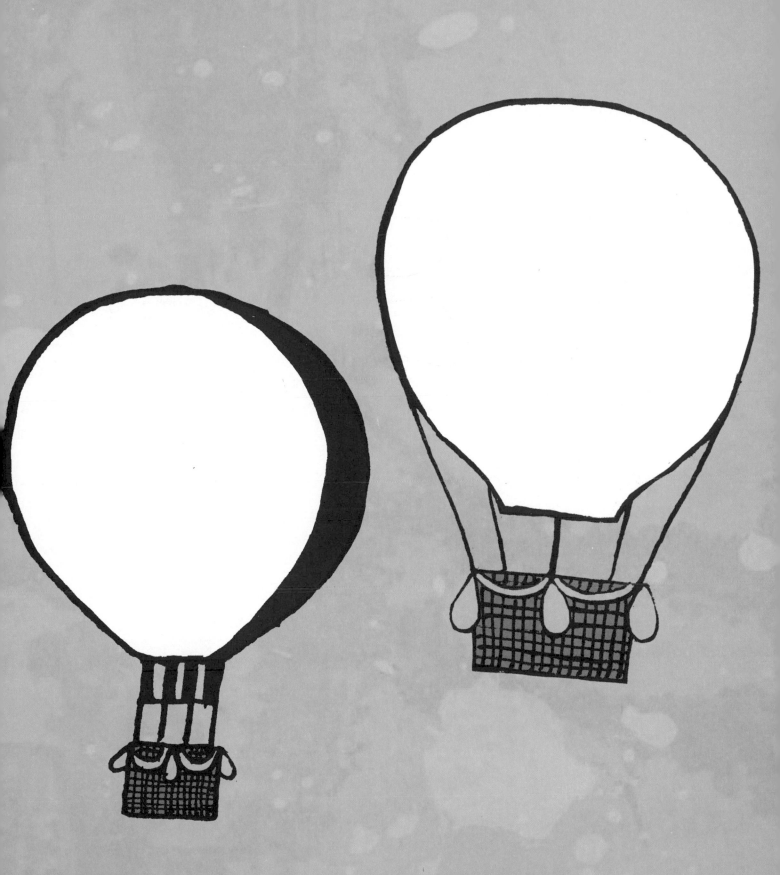

Draw your
favorite
song.

Draw the **SOUNDS** coming from this orchestra.

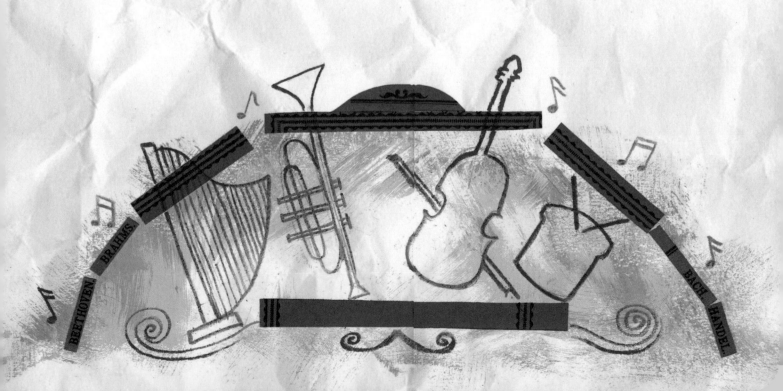

Draw a **backyard**

that can be seen through these patio doors.

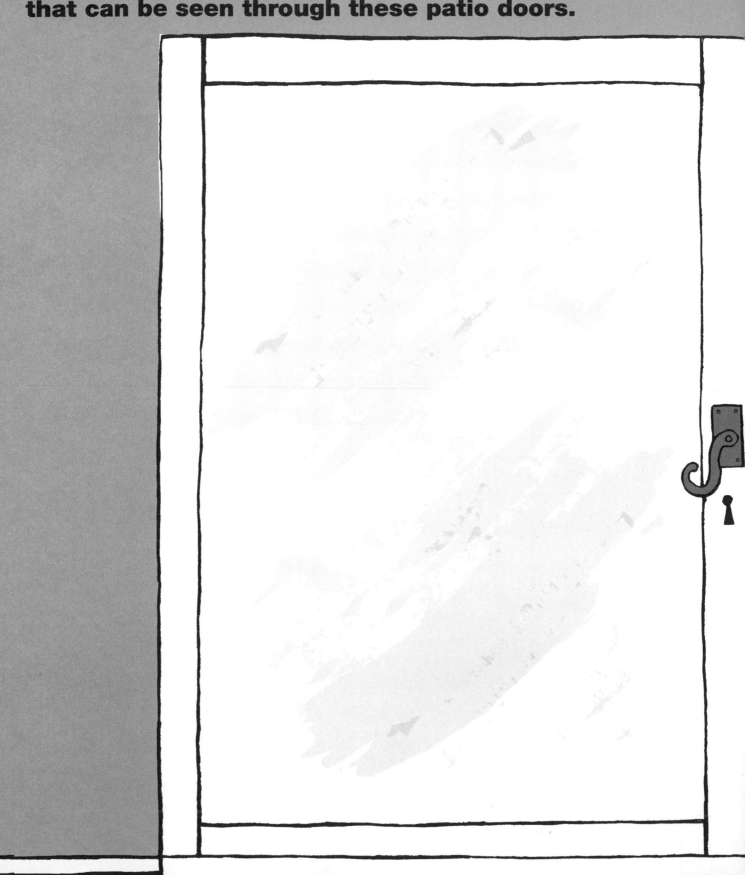

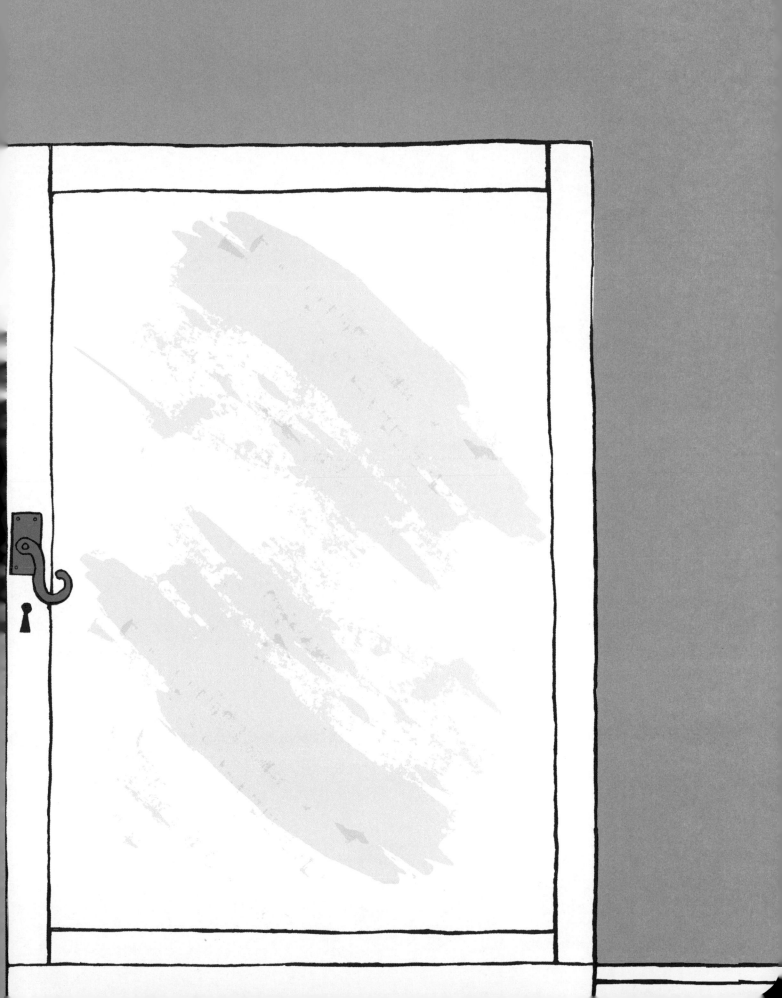

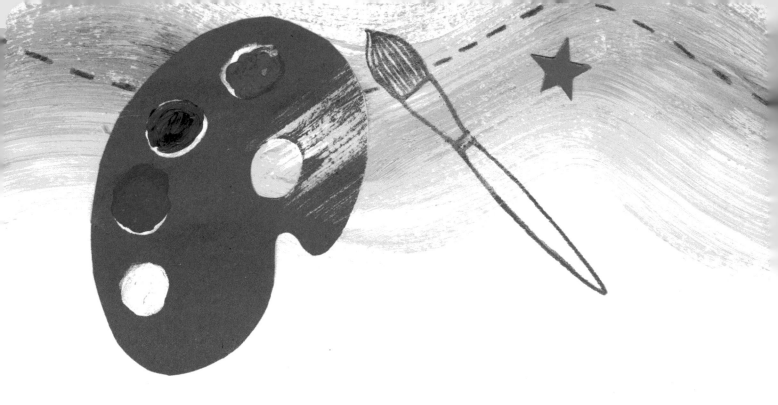

Fill these pages with

IDEAS.

Doodle frogs and flies.

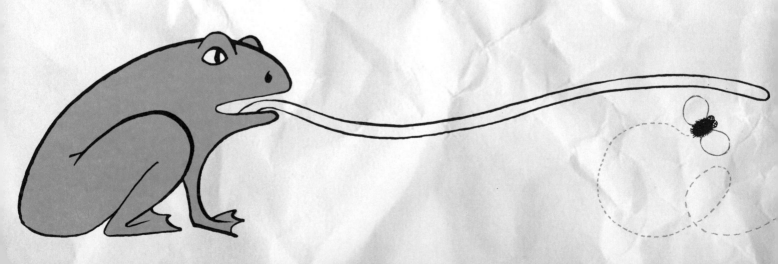

"Creativity is allowing yourself to make mistakes. Art is knowing which ones to keep." Scott Adams.